# The
# English Ballad

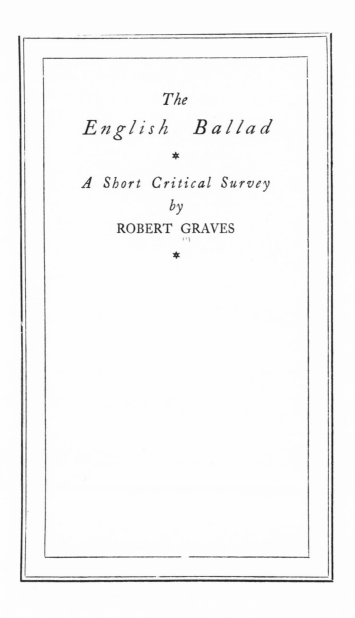

*The*

*English Ballad*

\*

*A Short Critical Survey*
*by*
ROBERT GRAVES

\*

**HASKELL HOUSE PUBLISHERS** Ltd.
*Publishers of Scarce Scholarly Books*
NEW YORK, N. Y. 10012
1971

First Published 1927

**HASKELL HOUSE PUBLISHERS** Ltd.
*Publishers of Scarce Scholarly Books*
280 LAFAYETTE STREET
NEW YORK. N. Y. 10012

Library of Congress Catalog Card Number: 70-155147

Standard Book Number 8383-1284-5

Printed in the United States of America

# INDEX OF BALLADS

Grateful acknowledgments are made to the editors and publishers of the source-books mentioned in the text, who have given permission for the inclusion of copyright material, and to the gentleman to whom this book is dedicated and to whom I owe a debt not to be measured in mere literary terms.

# INTRODUCTION

THE object of this brief survey is in the first place critical: though most of the examples are chosen for the strong appeal they usually have for ballad readers and singers, this does not claim to be an anthology of the best ballads in English. It is an attempt to trace the gradual development of the ballad from its earliest to its most advanced stages, and to discuss the causes of each differentiation. This is no easy task, as a moment's reflection will show, for such discussion implies a general agreement as to the true meaning of the word 'ballad.' And that is hard to arrive at, principally because most historians of the ballad have attempted to define it merely in terms of subject, length, metre, language, structure, or to confine it geographically and between certain dates in history. This method has involved so many contradictions and exceptions that confidence in it is now waning, and recent editors, though assuming that there *is* a consistent meaning to the word, have admitted that they rely rather on their intuition than on any formula in deciding what is a ballad and what is not; or else evade the issue by agreeing with the late Professor Ker that " In spite of Socrates and his logic we may venture to answer the question ' what is a ballad ? ' by saying—' Ballad is the *Milldams of Binnorie* and *Sir Patrick Spens* and *The Douglas Tragedy* and *Lord Randal* and *Childe Maurice* and things of that sort.' " But a more hopeful approach to the subject than either intuition or a bare examination of the form and size and geography of the ballad will be that of relating its development to social psychology: that is, discovering what organizations of society produce what sort of ' ballad.'

The actual word ' ballad ' came to England comparatively late in our ballad history and comparatively late in its own continental history. It is connected with the word ' ballet ' and originally meant a song or refrain intended as accompaniment to dancing, but later covered any song in which a group of people socially joined; after

7

transplantation to England it soon came to mean practically any song. So the *Song of Solomon* or *Song of Songs*,
which is not a sociable refrain at all but a personal love-
lyric, was once called *The Ballad of Ballads*. So also
Shakespeare speaks of the "Lover sighing like furnace,
With a woeful ballad made to his mistress' eyebrow." Let
us therefore remember that any specialized use that we
make of the word 'ballad' is unhistorical; that is, distinctions between the song and the narrative ballad, and
between the oral and the literary ballad, or similar distinctions, though convenient for our purposes, did not
exist until recent times. Let us also note that to treat of
what we are now calling the English ballad-proper as if
it had necessarily the same general history as the continental ballad-proper is not permissible. There is no
evidence that dancing has been a popular pastime or
social ceremony in these islands as long as it has been on
the warmer shores of the Mediterranean Sea: the English
ballad-proper has thriven most in the drinking-hall to the
clattering accompaniment of horn and pewter, and in field,
yard and ship as an encouragement for hard group-labour:
and labour songs even in the South are as ancient as the
dancing ballads. When the word 'ballad' was adopted by
English singers, though the association with dancing did not
survive, there remained latent in it the sense of *rhythmic
group action* whether in work or play. Wherever this sense
of group action remains in a ballad, let that ballad be distinguished as a ballad-proper; where it does not remain, other
labels must be found. For this ballad-proper is earliest in
poetic succession; from it derive all other so-called 'ballads,'
arising from many different organizations of society, and
only bound to the ballad-proper and to each other by the
most capricious of ties: indeed it is the common ancestor
of all varieties of verse.

The dictionary is the best place to go for a good highest-
common-factor definition of the whole ballad family: Dr.

Murray gives " a simple spirited poem in short stanzas in which some popular story is graphically told." But a definition wide enough to include poems so far apart as *Lord Randal*, *The Ancient Mariner* and *Felix kept on Walking* is almost valueless. Let us therefore first discuss the features of what literary historians agree to call the " early ballad in English," which is really the ballad-proper if these historians would admit that an early ballad may under certain circumstances be contemporary with civilized literature.[1]

1. The ballad-proper has no known author.

2. There is never an authoritative text of such a ballad.

3. It is incomplete without music, music of a repetitive kind that excites and sustains.

4. Though it may treat of Kings and Queens and notable figures in history, it is local, not cultural.

5. It is oral, not literary.

6. It is not highly advanced technically.

7. It does not moralize or preach or express any partisan bias.

8. It " begins in the last act " of the drama and moves to the final climax without stage directions.

Other common features are perhaps discoverable, but they will all be found intelligible in the light of the eight here detailed, and of this ninth which includes the other eight, that the *ballad-proper is best understood not primarily as a narrative poem or as a song, but as a song and chorus evolved by the group-mind of a community, a group-mind which is more than the sum of the individual minds that compose it, more than the conviction of the strongest or most active clique.*

9. This theory of the group-mind[2] being perhaps

---

[1] These characteristics are considered consecutively in the argument of this Introduction.

[2] See MacDougall's *Group Mind* and Rivers' *Instinct and the Unconscious*, both Cambridge University Press.

difficult to accept, a practical example of its working must
be given. In a primitive society, then, such as may still be
found in the less Europeanized islands of the South Seas,
the village or island community which is bound together
by far more intimate ties than any corresponding European
community comes to its practical decisions in a way that
travellers find very difficult to follow. There are no
minute books, no elected representatives of this or that
local interest, no elected chairman, none of the political,
religious or inter-class intrigue and counter-intrigue from
which parish or district councils in Western Europe are
seldom free and from which indeed they derive their chief
vitality. Opinions for or against any project are given,
but no count of hands is taken. When the topic has been
exhausted there is a pause, then another topic is started:
and the European is surprised to discover that the community has already, by what he might call telepathy or
occult instinct, decided what action to take. What has
happened is that the group-mind has come into being and
the individuals as such have disappeared, so that a common
decision and a common realization of that decision is
possible: which is just what constantly happens with herds
of deer or flocks of sheep or birds. But where there are
national and international institutions, central government, a complex system of trade, a constantly changing
population, it is idle to expect a small community to act
like this. The diversity of religion, politics, occupation,
class, wealth, education makes it all but impossible for the
individuals to have a whole-hearted respect for the small
community of which they are, by residence or other quali-
fication, members. When surprising circumstances occasionally do bind the civilized local group strongly together
(but this will imply a partial breakdown of civilization and
a weakening of class and other distinctions in face of a
common danger or calamity), and when therefore the
group-mind does momentarily appear and the individual

formerly out of touch do act in concert as a single unit, this phenomenon is afterwards accounted for with great difficulty by the individuals re-established as individuals. One of the chief reasons why people talk so little now about the surprising social changes that temporarily appeared during the late War, is that they are bewildered and ashamed to think how often they sank their individualities in the national, local or regimental group-mind: for to keep one's individuality is by most Englishmen, at any rate of the educated classes, considered to be somehow a greater thing than good citizenship. This is the fundamental difference between primitive and modern society, that under civilization the community has broken up into a number of individual centres loosely bound by bureaucratic administration and settles its disputes or common policy by majority-voting or bayonet-superiority. In politics this individualistic idea is expressed by the general horror of socialism and communism, in religion by profuse sectarianism, while in poetry and music, which is the point to which this argument has been moving, about the only quality which modern critics agree to acknowledge necessary for great art is this ' individuality,' which usually implies the poet's bid for personal ascendancy over the slower-moving part of the community.

Professor Sir Walter Raleigh used to deride altogether the possibility of communal ballad-composition. He suggested as a practical test that a number of even highly gifted people should be shut up together in a room and asked to compose a ballad. Would not the result, he asked, be farcical? A poem, he insisted, is a one-man business. He pointed to *Sir Patrick Spens* and asked whether there was anyone who could seriously suggest that it was not originally the work of a single hand. These criticisms were quite in order, for the case for communal composition has lately been overstated, but they do not affect the main issue. It is true that the highly gifted people

selected at random and shut up to compose a ballad, as
juries are impanelled to decide their 'guilty' or 'not
guilty,' would immediately create a Parish Council
atmosphere of suppressed conflict, each individual or small
combination of individuals trying to impress the piece with
a particular character. The ballad would probably get
written, as even Parish Councils usually get their business
done when the hour gets too late to make further intrigue
worth while, but what a ballad it would be! It might
likely enough contain witty flashes, but being merely a
compromise between rival characters it would not have
the harmonious flow which we expect from the ballad-
proper. It would be self-conscious, it would have no
dignity, *it would not be the work of a group but of a number
of separate minds,* which is a very different thing. The
more highly gifted the individuals, the more nugatory the
result which might be expected. And in this case the
occasion for the composition of the ballad would be forced:
though the ballad-proper is not always at a highly emotional
pitch, it flows inevitably like a stream and cannot be forced
uphill.

Moreover, to give *Sir Patrick Spens* as an example of
communal composition would not be fair, for it certainly
began as a one-man poem: though in the secondary sense
it *is* a ballad-proper, for its numerous variants prove that
the community early adopted it as its own and remoulded
it, and so *Sir Patrick Spens* became anonymous.

(1) Anonymity in the present structure of society
usually implies that the author is ashamed of his authorship
or afraid of consequences if he reveals himself; but in a
primitive society is due just to carelessness of the author's
name. This carelessness may be only on the part of the
community; but in conditions where the poet-musician
has not yet become a person of great distinction it is also
on the part of the author. For there must be some original
author who in the intoxication of fellowship starts the

ballad going and even orders its general direction, but the
peculiarity of communal composition is that this original
author is merely acting as spokesman for the group and
when the ballad is complete will not claim it as his own.
The ballad is important, the group is important, but the
individual counts for little.    Rudimentary balladry is
common among groups of small children, and in such
cases, too, it will be noticed that no child, unless one of
sophisticated age is condescending to help, will claim
authorship of the sing-song:   no one remembers who
added which phrases to the common store.

As the closeness and intimacy of the primitive group is
gradually dissolved by the civilizing process, there appears
an accepted chorus leader who specializes in ballad impro-
visation and, though still a member of the group, begins
to compose ballads on his own without feeling the stimulus
of fellowship necessary, but studies to make them effective
when the occasion for singing them comes.   Then their
test as ballads proper is whether they are accepted by the
group, remembered and subsequently recast into variants
which suit it better than the originals.

(2) At this stage the ballad is still everybody's song.
That is why there is never any actual correct text of a
ballad-proper: singers are allowed to alter it to their liking,
and though some variants are earlier in date or more wide-
spread in popularity or more poetical than others, no single
version must be regarded as ' the right one ' in an absolute
sense.   The poem that has lost or mislaid its individual
author and found a new author in the community begins
a quite different life:   in the end has all its bardic angu-
larities smoothed away as pebbles are rounded in a stony
stream.   In this final stage it becomes much admired by
modern literary ballad-writers, who cannot in their own
compositions achieve the same smoothness even with
grindstone and file.

Of the more primitive ballads which are of communal

inspiration from the first, few are nowadays of great poetic appeal except to groups of young children, to sailors on sailing ships, to soldiers on the march, or in similar cases where the social organization is of a simple kind. Such ballads consist mostly in simple variants on a suggestive theme: as, for instance, the statement that " London Bridge is broken down "; after which the natural question arises how it shall be repaired and various suggestions are made, of which one at last is accepted as satisfactory, but even then complications arise and have to be adjusted. *London Bridge* is a children's song, perhaps first a chorus for London apprentices. It is not a literary composition. The nautical problem: *What shall we do with the drunken sailor ?* is treated in much the same way as that of London Bridge. The question: *Who killed Cock Robin ?* sets the group embroidering the theme with tragi-comic reference to one bird after another. *There was a pig went out to dig* directs their fancy through a course of domesticated animals and the different seasonal occupations of agriculture. *The Maid Freed from the Gallows* is an example of the same sort of process. And there are numerous cumulative ballads like—

> *In the wood*
> *There stood a hill,*
> *And on that hill*
> *There grew a tree*
> *And on that tree*
> *There grew a bough ;*

and *On the first day of Christmas my true love sent to me a partridge in a pear tree ;* and the famous Yorkshire ballad *Ilkla Moor* (in which the man went courting without a hat and caught cold, and died, and was buried, and decayed, and was eaten by worms, and they eaten by ducks and so on), where the progress is simple and secure. Such ballads can even be historical in giving the main incidents of rise and fall in the lives of the great: the ballad *Boney was a warrior* is a good instance. But in structure all such ballads are readily distinguished from ballads of the type of *Sir Patrick Spens* or the *Wife of Usher's Well*, where the narrative slowly works up to a passionate climax and almost always ends quietly with a "dying close."

A stage further in the development of the ballad-singing community beyond the chorus-leader stage finds the bard definitely outside the group: he begins to claim special privileges of honour and wealth hitherto only accorded to the warrior and the priest. He becomes in fact a professional, and either visits from group to group or attaches himself permanently to his local overlord. Once the intimate connexion between the balladist and the group is broken, the ballad tends to become more and more sophisticated and individualistic; the chorus no longer the chief part of the ballad becomes a mere polite accompaniment to assure the balladist that he has his audience with him. The balladist can no longer plunge straight into his song, but the lack of real contact between him and his hearers makes it necessary to capture their attention and sympathy by an introductory stanza informing them of his intentions. The bard has climbed to a slight social eminence from which true intimacy with the people is difficult. It is noticeable that a grand attempt is being made at the present day in Soviet Russia to discredit all modern European literature as *bourgeois*, that is poetry of private commercial enterprise, and to recapture the secret of communal poetry, the readiest instance of which is the ballad-proper. The success of this campaign, which is inspired by the Government, will depend on whether Russia is a true communal state or not: if the Government is, as many assert, a despotism unwillingly borne by the people, and if the desire for private enterprise still remains everywhere uncrushed, there will be no such

communal poetry.  But if the Government is representative of the people and communism can become a habit,
communal art may be expected as readily as communal
ploughing.  It is true that even the chief in the primitive
community is merely the chosen military representative
and makes no individualistic claim at the expense of his
fellows; but it is a big step in history to go back behind
private enterprise.

The professional bard was already an institution among
the Anglo-Saxons, the Danes and the Normans when they
invaded our shores and almost certainly among the earlier
inhabitants.  But though enjoying the favour of princes
and notables he had not supplanted the amateur within
the group.  In the well-known account of the poet
Caedmon's first poetic inspiration (about the year 670), it
is recorded that when in the hall of Whitby Abbey, where
Caedmon was a lay-brother, the harp went round from
hand to hand, he rose for shame and retired to his stables,
not being able to take a part.  This Abbey society was
plainly independent of the professional, though acquainted
with his lays, and in remoter and poorer parts of the
country the harp would be heard seldom and visits from
the travelling professional would be rare.  So it will be
wrong to suggest that at such and such a date in English
history the communal chorus-song everywhere gives place
to the minstrel[1] ballad: the chorus-song persists outside the
few cultural centres where the minstrels are able to find
a living, in the same way as common rights persist in the
country long after they have disappeared in the towns.
But it can be observed that the chorus-song is affected
more and more by the minstrel ballad, and that the
minstrel ballads, imperfectly remembered or deliberately
simplified by the remote community there, lose their
individualistic character.

[1] The word minstrel, from the Latin *ministralis* or attendant, implies a
patron to whom the balladist is attached.

For the appearance of the professional bard, the *scop* or
'shaper of words,' as the Anglo-Saxons called him, the
*scald* or 'loud singer,' as the Northmen called him, is
marked by differentiations of the communal chorus-song,
which are all towards individualism. At first these will
be chiefly compositions celebrating the prowess and liber-
ality of the bard's patron and his ancestors. Then will
come other narrative ballads to instruct and amuse. Later
the personal 'song' will appear, for the professional will
exercise his gift of character-study in mimicking the feelings and actions of the principal character in a ballad.
This central core of narrative history is concentrated upon
as a popular tit-bit, elaborated with metaphor, and enriched
with general thoughts on love, fate and religion. But
metaphor and moralizing are rare in early bardic compositions where war is the chief communal interest: they
come only with settled conditions of cultivation and trade.
*Waly, Waly* is a good example of a song that has thus
broken away from a ballad and set up on its own. These
songs are half-way to the lyric, where the narrative
interest and the communal setting give place to private
enterprise in philosophy, religion or art. The character
speaking in the song is definitely outside the group to
whom it is addressed, and usually, like *Loving Mad Tom*,
asking for sympathy. But there is also a variety of
the communal song in the first personal singular, such
as *Jack o' Diamonds*, where the singer is proclaiming
himself a typical if unfortunate member of the cowboy
fraternity: or *Blow the Man Down*, where he is a typical
if tough seaman; or *I want to go Home*, where he is a
typical if war-weary soldier. This is a 'we' song rather
than an 'I' song, but presupposes the individualistic
tradition.

(3) The ballad is incomplete without an exciting and
repetitive music. This book is really incomplete without
the music: unfortunately it has not been found practicable

B

to include it.  But no lover of these ballads should fail to
acquaint himself with the collections of ballads with their
music made by the late Cecil Sharpe for the English Folk
Song Society and similar compilations of the Welsh,
Scottish and Irish Societies, and should, if possible, have
a real singing familiarity with them.  It is probable that
the drum was the first musical accompaniment of the
primitive ballad, but whether drum or harp or the voice
of the chorus leader is used, the power of the music lies
in subordinating the individuals to the group rhythm, after
which the singing and elaboration of the ballad becomes
a communal act:  the group gets worked up to a fertile
creative state, the repetition of the musical refrain being
a spur to further efforts.  Now as we have observed the
gradual breakdown of the communal ballad when the group
leader begins to specialize as a poet, so also with the music
of the ballad.  The more the bard (who is musician as well
as balladist) elaborates his musical accompaniment, the
less suitable does it become for its purpose:  the group-
singing becomes subservient to the musician's skill with
the harp or lute.  The balladist soon gets outside the group
and sets up as a professional:  the refrain becomes perfunc-
tory and then disappears altogether.  Though at first the
bard combines both trades, music and poetry, after a time
poetry and music begin to specialize on their own.  We
cna see the turning-point in the magnificent lutanist song-
books published between 1590 and 1643 (the exact period
which saw the differentiation of the Blank Verse drama
from the old interludes and morality plays) where the lute
gradually takes the greater share of the partnership to
itself:  with few exceptions the words of the songs verge
on the trivial, yet seldom are quite worthless.  They are
still performing a useful part, but they suggest the faithful
friend of the hero in a novel or epic, a foil to greatness.
In what are still called 'ballad-concerts' to-day the
emphasis is entirely on the music ; the words have sunk

to the degrading position of unpaid drudges. But modern ballad poetry has meanwhile specialized on its own and come to do without the help of even a drum or tin whistle. The rise of individualism has meant narrower and narrower specialization: so that co-operation between the specialized poet and the specialized musician has become practically impossible. One of the two always insists on dominating the other.

But we are anticipating somewhat. The specialized poet and musician are town products at an advanced stage in cultural history. Let us return to the ballad minstrel who avoiding cultural centres is still touring the shires: he practises undisturbed for a long period until the town culture begins to invade the country. His technique changes little, and his ballad themes only very gradually: many of them are drawn from popular legend of immense age: ethnologists quarrel about the origin of these themes, but they certainly occur in the folk-lore and balladry of numerous nations both in Europe and Asia. Others are drawn from Biblical history or legend, and a third variety celebrates stirring events of recent history. It is only at a late stage of the minstrel ballad that subjects are taken from books. *Bruton Town* possibly derives from Boccaccio's *Tale of the Pot of Basil*, but it is rare for the literary ballad to be popularly accepted and to become a ballad-proper, as *Bruton Town* perhaps did by surviving in oral tradition.

(4) and (5). Here we come to an important point. A ballad, though it may treat of Kings and Queens and other notables, is local, not cultural. It is oral, not literary. These two statements are closely allied in sense. Where there is a national culture based on a confederation of tribes and small communities, the strongest, wealthiest or best situated member of the confederation will soon establish itself as a centre of government and consequently as a seat of musical and literary culture. The balladists who have collected under the protection of the

King are well provided for, and have leisure to elaborate their arts with the aid of pen and ink.

(6) It has been noted that the ballad-proper is not highly advanced in technique: by 'advanced technique' is meant complicated verse-forms, the ingenious use of metaphor and allegory, and a presentation of ideas which is 'poetical' before it is poetic, 'artistic' before it is imaginative, 'musical' before it is intended for singing. The complicated training which ancient court bards had to undergo did in most cases no doubt stifle the poetic impulse. It is recorded that in ancient Ireland the bardic students had among other rigorous tasks to lie all night in a coffin-like box with heavy weights resting on their body, or for hours in a bath of cold water, and with these aids to concentration were set to compose formal odes in metres of a complication seldom since rivalled. Yet the greater spirits were not broken by even this apprenticeship and could write poems of great force and integrity even within the rigorous bonds of consonantal sequence, chain-rhyme and difficult rhythm. A poem whose poetic force is not spent in the process of achieving these technical feats is to be distinguished from a ballad like *Sir Patrick Spens* that has no such technical ambitions, but does what it attempts very finely. This specialization in technique, which is generally known as 'cultural progress,' is in the first instance a means of winning the admiration of a prince or noble patron where there are other less skilled competitors. But once a technical standard is set and competition is keen it is extremely difficult to return to the rougher forms without antagonizing the audience. So the advance continues in proportion to the social distinction or payment which skilful technique can earn; until it culminates in forms like the Welsh four-line *Englyn* which is guarded by scores of inhibitive rules and which does not sound very pleasing to the uninitiated ear even when it is triumphantly achieved.

(7) The specialization in form is matched by a specialization in treatment of the subject. The cultural ballad
is used didactically to express some religious or philosophic
point. It is even sometimes allegorical: the ballad-proper
does not moralize or preach or express any strong partisan
bias. The song and the story alone are considered. The
singers identify themselves with the characters, and the
only comment on the story is the tone in which each
character speaks. Moralizing or preaching in a ballad is
a sign that the bard is definitely outside the group and is
in touch with culture. A partisan bias is incompatible
with group-action.

(8) The ballad-proper begins in the last act of the drama
and moves to the final climax without stage directions.
This tendency disappears in the cultural narrative, because the method of education is to arrange the poetic
meal in logical sequence from the soup to the savoury and
to connect each course with the next by due announce-
ment. And the cultural balladist is historian, not pro-
tagonist in a group-drama: he has lost the group. These
cultural forms will be strengthened and perpetuated by
letters. Letters are at first the monopoly of the priests
and the court bards, who are the historians and the legal
recorders. It is considered unsuitable and even discredit-
able for any one else to be able to read and write. But
reading and writing soon prove their usefulness in com-
merce, and the centre of government becoming also the
commercial centre an educated class soon rises which
gets the habit of reading books for pleasure and instruction.
But hundreds of years pass before education spreads to the
military and land-owning classes, and hundreds of years
pass after that before the manual worker learns to read.
The unlearned classes are thus left to enjoy the earlier
culture of oral tradition and are quite out of touch intel-
lectually with the learned classes; while that is so the
ballad-proper and the highly advanced lyric can live side

by side.   But as soon as the unlearned classes consider that
they are being exploited by the lawyers and other representatives of the centralized state, are not given the rewards
to which their labour, as they hold, entitles them, they
think of education as a powerful weapon which they themselves would like to handle.   But education means an
entirely new vocabulary and system of thought, and the
inevitable consequence of the unlettered local man
arming himself with cultural book-learning is that he
despises as trivial all his ancestral ballads and songs,
and his former associates who still remain unlettered:
he takes pains to educate his children in the same
way.

The ballad-proper is poisoned by the blessings of letters
as surely as river-fish are by the blessings of tarred roads,
its wings are clogged as the wings of sea-fowl are by the
blessings of naval oil fuel.   But even before the manual
worker learns to read the improving classics with which
he aims to better his social and financial position, there
have been other influences at work undermining the ballad.
The beginning of the end of the ballad-proper is when no
more are composed: and it is a fact that in England the
ballad-proper gradually ceased to be composed after Tudor
times.   It was not only that the organization of the rural
community had been altered by national consolidation
and culture, but that along with the travelling pedlar
and cheap-jack from the towns came a new arrival, the
ballad seller.   The ballad seller was the man who ousted
the travelling bard, and his way was cleared by legislation
against the bards, who no longer were held in their ancient
respect, having lost the patronage of the wealthier classes:
the ballad seller came from the towns, armed not with
educated poems but with ' broadsheets ' or ' broadsides,'
narrative verses in a rough imitation of the old ballad style
such as the townsmen thought would be acceptable in the
country.   Here is a picture from Henry Chettle's *Kind*

*Harte's Dreame* of a last minstrel who bewailed his trade
taken by these new-comers:

" He was an odd old fellow low of stature : his head was
covered with a round cap, his body with a side-skirted tawny
coat, his legs and feet trussed up in leather buskins, his grey
hairs and furrowed face witnessed his age, his treble-viol
in his hand assured me of his profession. On which (by his
continual sawing having but one string) he gave me a hunt's-
up. . . . I remembered him to be no other than old Anthony
Now-Now."

He complained that " times are changed and men are
changed in the times," that, though he was one of the
few ballad minstrels excepted by Elizabeth's stringent law
against able-bodied rogues and vagabonds, the law had
not benefited him at all. Players and fiddlers were liable
by law to the usual punishment of vagabondage, being
branded in the ear, unless they were employed by a respect-
able citizen: the pitches being therefore cleared, the
Stationers in London found it profitable to take on apprentices and, instead of teaching them the stationer's trade,
send them out singing and selling ballads in the neighbour-
ing shires. " Is it not lamentable that such a flock
of runagates should overspread the face of this land
as at this time it doth? " says Anthony Now-Now. He
describes:

" the blushless faces of certain Babies, sons to one Barnes most
frequenting Bishop's Stafford. . . . The one in a squeaking treble,
the other in an ale-blown bass carrol out such ribaldry as chaste
ears abhor to hear and modesty hath no tongue to utter, . . .
while the old ale-knight their dad breaks out in admiration and
sends straggling customers to admire the roaring of his sons :
where . . . they hear no better matter than the lascivious under-
songs of *Watkin's Ale, The Carman's Whistle, Chopping Knives*
and *Friar Foxtail*, and that with such odious and detested bold-
ness as if there be any one line in those lewd songs than other

more abominable, that one with a double repetition is loudly
bellowed, as for example of the friar and the nun :—

" ' He whipt her with a fox's tail,' sings Barnes minor.
" ' And he whipt her with a fox's tail,' sings Barnes major.
' O brave Boys,' saith Barnes Maximus.  The father leaps, the
lubbers roar, the people run, the Devil laughs, God lours, and
good men weep."

And here is another burlesqued ballad seller, Shakespeare's Autolycus of the *Winter's Tale*.  He was protected
by his pedlar's licence against the vagabondage laws.

CLOWN. What hast here ?  ballads ?
MOPSA. Pray now, buy some.  I love a ballad in print o' life,
for then we are sure they are true.
AUTOLYCUS. Here's a ballad of a fish that appeared upon the
west on Wednesday the fourscore of April, forty thousand fathom
above water and sung this ballad against the hard hearts of maids.
It is thought she was a woman and was turned into a cold fish
for she would not exchange kisses with one that loved her.  The
ballad is very pitiful and as true.
DORCAS. Is it true, think you ?
AUTOLYCUS. Five justices' hands at it, and witnesses more
than my pack will hold.
CLOWN. Lay it by : another.
AUTOLYCUS. This is a passing merry one and goes to the tune
of *Two maids wooing a man*.  There's scarce a maid westward
but she sings it : 'tis in request, I can tell you.

The account is not much exaggerated.  A ballad in the
Shirburn collection of broadsheets is entitled *A most
miraculous strange and trewe ballad of a maid now dwelling
at the town of Meurs in Dutchland, that hath not taken any
food this* 16 *years and is not yet neither hungry nor thirsty :
the which maid hath lately been presented to the Lady
Elizabeth the King's daughter of England.  This song
was made by the maid herself and now translated into
English.*

These ballads were, as the *Winter's Tale* quotation shows, set to familiar tunes, not given new ones, which marks an important stage in popular ballad history. The story was getting the upper hand of the music. These broadsheets were indeed the chief means of circulating news of national importance or journalistic interest. Anthony Now-Now was not fair in describing all of them as insolently ribald: many of them took the line that the gutter-Press takes to-day, exploiting indecency and scurrility under a pretence of deep moral indignation, and many like the broadsheet ballad of *The Children in the Wood*, the first appearance of that familiar tale, were innocency itself. The broadside did a good trade for two centuries after Shakespeare's death: until the days of Charles Dickens the walls of inns were regularly papered with them. The newspaper, sold at sixpence or a shilling, was not yet a rival; the end of the broadside's popularity only came with national education, when it became possible for the penny and halfpenny newspaper to be sold at a profit in country districts. The broadsheet still survives, but as precariously as Anthony Now-Now himself; coronations, brutal murders or cricket matches being the most hopeful occasions for its appearance.

The unlearned country folk and the poorer classes of the towns were not the only public for the broadsheet ballad. A distinct variety, the political broadside, had a great vogue in the eighteenth century. Whigs and Tories both realized the value of the satiric ballad as a weapon in election campaigns or other political occasions, and the ballad lustily roared in mug-houses and gentlemen's clubs regained some of its communal character. But though the influence of drink, tobacco and a common party enthusiasm made sociability easy, the proceedings at these political sing-songs were regulated by a president who sat in an arm-chair some steps higher than the rest of the company to keep the room in order; proving that the community was not too intimately bound. In a ballad, *The Club Room*, we see this president at work:—

> In my club room so great
> When I'm seated in state
> At the head of the table I shine.
> With hammer in hand
> Zounds! how I command
> As I push round the bumpers of wine.
> Then after we've toasted the health of the King
> Mr. Briscket the butcher is called on to sing.

He sang, and seems to have often finished his song under the table. These political ballads originated, like their present-day successors the election cartoons, from party headquarters; but there were no doubt local additions improvised by Mr. Briscket and his friends, highly laughable in character and much applauded, but forgotten again when heads had cleared. The broadsheet ballad was not always propagandist or journalistic in the most blatant sense of that word, for often the stationer-printers whom Anthony Now-Now described as " Devil's Instruments, intruders into Printing's mystery, by whom that excellent Art is not smally slandered, the Government of the Estate not a little blemished nor Religion in the least measure hindered," struck off versions of Anthony's own ballads for the convenience of districts where they had not yet circulated. Though these versions are generally 'improved' by a thorough smoothing out of the metre, more 'poetical' diction, and a circumstantial modernizing of the story so as to make it acceptable as a news item, this is not always the case; the printer often finding it more convenient to record the ballad as he heard it sung. And occasionally the author of the newer broadsides had a poetic power which the lowness of the life he celebrates enhances rather than obscures. The ballads of *Loving Mad Tom* and of *The Night before Larry was Stretched* can hardly be too highly praised.

The broadsheet seller put the ballad minstrel out of trade, but that is not to say that the old oral ballad itself was thereby killed. The journalistic or political broadsheet was never intended to outlast its topical appeal, and seldom did, while recent researches of the Folk Song Societies show that the old oral ballad has surprisingly survived in the countryside to our day and versions are found most unexpectedly in places like the East End of London, and the Appalachian Mountains of America where the early settlers brought them. But, the ballad minstrel being gone, few pieces in the old vein were composed after Elizabethan times: the towns had their topical verses, and in the country there were few events of dramatic importance to be celebrated. Common danger appears to be one of the chief formative influences of the ballad-proper: and danger, except the dangers of sickness, tempest and famine, had largely been ruled out of country life. There remained only the humorous ballad: and the great Nonconformist religious movements in the early part of last century swept away a good deal of the broader pieces. The ones that survived popularly were witty rather than humorous. But the humorous ballad no less than other varieties was influenced by the broadsheet; there are few later pieces of the type of *The Old Cloak* or *Get out and Bar the Door, Oh !* Though *Wednesbury Cocking* is unusually free from Grub-street influence, it has characteristics obvious enough which prevent it from being called a ballad-proper. Clearly it is written by a cynic who has no real part in the community and is hardly a song which would be popularly accepted.

So for more recent examples of the ballad-proper in English we must look outside England to the new territories in America and Australia, where groups of English-speaking colonists bound together by common dangers and interests and separated by the sea from civilization are able to form an intense communal life. The south-west of the

United States fifty years ago was especially rich in ballads;
but well-planned and standardized towns have now sprung
up where the cowboy then built his camp fire, and national
American culture has triumphed both in music and poetry.
In Australia the up-country ballad has likewise been killed
by the gramophone and other missionaries of culture. But
the trappers in the far north-east of Canada still sing their
long melancholy ballads in English and Colonial French.
Nor has the emancipation of the American negro and his
recent great educational advance yet succeeded in killing
the negro ballad. Though the white man seldom finds in
these ballads much poetic distinction he can hardly deny
their musical strength. They were chiefly composed in
pre-Abolition days when the plantation gangs were bound
together closely by a stringent slavery and a common
Christian fervour. They are ballads-proper in every sense
and mostly begin with a simple religious statement such as
" Good News! The Chariots are coming," or " Ezekiel
saw a wheel," from which the loose structure of the communal ballad develops in the usual way.

Another field for the later growth of the English ballad-
proper was the long-voyaging sailing-ship. The ship's
company before the age of steam and rapid voyages was
one of the closest communities to be found in civilization,
and a sympathetic study of the ' forebitters,' which are
ballads of leisure for use between watches, and of the
' chanties,' which are ballads of work, will help a good
deal towards understanding the early history of the land
ballad.

Mr. Frank Shay writes in a foreword to his useful
*Iron Men and Wooden Ships* :—

" There are many kinds of chanties, a chanty for every duty,
and the order to *heave and chanty* brought redoubled efforts and
made them lighter. Literally there are but three kinds of
chanties : capstan chanties, used in warpings or weighing anchor
or hoisting sails ; the halyard, or long-drag chanty, used at top-

sails and top-gallant sails ; the sheet, tack, and bowline chanties, more often known as short-drag chanties, were used when the fore, main, or cross-jack sheets were hauled aft and bowlines tautened and made fast. Other chanties, such as hand-over-hand and pumping chanties, explain themselves. The ballads were, as a rule, called *forebitters*, taking their name from the stage or platform on which the singer or soloist took his place, the fore-bitts, a handy construction of wood near the foremast through which many of the main ropes were fed. In this manner he was raised some three or four feet above his fellows, who squatted about on kegs and coils of rope. He had no accompaniment, though often the watch joined in on the chorus. Neither chanties nor forebitters were ever written down. They varied greatly according to the soloist and chantyman. They began with regulation verses and carried on as long as the task lasted. If further verses were required the chantyman improvised, taking, very often, some incident that had occurred on shore and with which the crew was familiar. He had only to trust to his imagination : the versification was simple and there was much latitude as to rhymes and metre, and most of the airs would sound monotonous to ears accustomed to more highly developed music."

As happens in all communities where women are absent, the sea-ballad is much concerned with thoughts of them, and varies strangely between the obscene and the over-sentimental. The cowboy ballad is another example of this tendency. Steam and wireless killed the sea-ballad, but it survived latest in the old-style tramp steamer, which with her adventurous combats with heavy weather and unprofitable freights inspired her company with some of the bitter affection that crews had once felt for the square-rigged sailing-ship. Moreover, her officers were nearly always ex-sailing-ship men.

A remarkable revival of the ballad-proper in modern times, not a literary or sentimental revival, took place in the trenches in the early part of the late War. The history of the revival is interesting because these ballads

went in a short period through the various stages we have
noticed in the general history of the ballad.  In the winter
of 1914–1915, when the greater part of the original
expeditionary force had been put out of action, when the
new Kitchener divisions had not yet come out and the
ranks of the original units had been filled with old reser-
vists and raw troops, discipline in the Old Army sense was
considerably weakened.  The non-commissioned officers
were newly promoted and the junior officers untrained,
so that, hardships and dangers being excessive and the
smaller units thrown very much on their own resources,
there was for a time a fraternization of all ranks which was
inconceivable in the old regular army, and sternly discouraged in all regiments at a later stage in the War.

This temporary change in the structure of the military
group led to remarkable instances of communal action, as
opposed to action organized by orders from above: fortu-
nately this communal action took the form of attack and
defence more often than that of flight.  At this stage
appeared the ballad, both the 'forebitter,' so to speak, for
singing in billets, and the 'chanty' for marching.  Musical
instruments there were none beyond the mouth organ or
a rare concertina, nor were there *Liederbüchen* available
like those supplied by the thoughtful German Higher
Command.  *Tipperary* soon palled, and there was a
scarcity of other suitable ballads; perhaps the three most
popular marching songs of that date were *Who killed Cock
Robin ?*, *One man went to mow, went to mow a meadow*,
both ancient cumulative songs, and the American Civil
War ballad, *John Brown's Body*.  The new ballads were
composed nobody remembers by whom.  In a battalion
of the 1st Division with which the writer was serving in
the spring of 1915 there were a number of ballads sung
which with variants both of music and words spread
through the New Army and Territorial Divisions as they
came over.  Most of these were subversive of military

discipline, such as the well-known *I want to go Home* and *The Top of the Dixie Lid* ballad. When the line held by these brave but (from the Staff's point of view) unsoldier-like troops was finally consolidated, and discipline restored in a stricter sense, the ballad changed. Comforts of all sorts were arranged for men resting behind the line, among them regular entertainments. Men who had been foremost in improvising additions to the new ballads were chosen to form brigade and divisional concert parties for permanent duty. The chorus leader, in fact, became a bard. At this stage the ballad became far more sophisticated; the ballads of *Tickler's Jam* and of the *Jolly old Sergeant Major*, sung in Y.M.C.A. and Church Army huts to piano accompaniment, are readily distinguishable from their ruder predecessors. They were censored by authority, and the singer seldom wanted to be returned to trench duty for expressing in his compositions any feeling of despondency or weariness of war. Then came a whole flood of cultural balladry of a patriotic nature from England and gramophones and even, a few miles behind the line, concert parties of civilians, male and female. The ballad-proper retreated to the less-centralized theatres of war in the East, and only lingered in France in a few battalions or corps where disciplined moral was not particularly strong.

Mention has not yet been made of the literary ballad, which is merely one of the many varieties of verse developed in cultural centres, distinguishable from the lyric, the epic, the satire, the poetic drama by its form rather than by its psychology. It will be a narrative poem in short stanzas and without music. Cowper's *John Gilpin*, Hood's *Eugene Aram*, Browning's *How they Brought the Good News*, are literary ballads in this sense. But these, which are merely well-written developments of the broadsheet, are distinguishable from the mock-antique ballads written in the style of the ballad-proper and mostly based

on a study of Percy's *Reliques of English Poetry*, in some
ways the most important book of poetry published in the
eighteenth century.  In 1765, when the *Reliques* appeared,
serious poetry had practically been limited to the heroic
couplet, correctly-scanning blank verse and a few other
metres of iambic base; politeness and decorum had limited
also the possible subject-matter of poetry, so that these
"gusty verses of a ruder age" which Percy had edited
from an ancient folio manuscript of ballads-proper and
early metrical romances, came as a revelation and a relief
to jaded readers of Pope and his school.  The communistic
feeling of the ballad-proper was recognized, and the cult
of the ballad in England went hand in hand with a liberal
feeling towards the French Revolution.  The Romantic
revivalists—Burns, Coleridge, Shelley, Keats, Wordsworth—were all profoundly indebted to Percy's collection.
When the second revolutionary wave came on Europe in
the middle of the nineteenth century, the beginning of
modern socialism, the ballad was again revived by the
young English revolutionaries of that day, the chief poet
of whom was William Morris.

Percy was probably not profoundly attached to these
ballads as poetry: rather he was an amateur antiquarian,
and the success of his publication surprised him a good deal.
But the *Reliques* enabled him to change his name from
Piercy to Percy and to win an acknowledgment of kinship
from the great Northumberland family whom the *Battle
of Otterbourne* glorifies, and in the end brought him a
bishopric.  The only trouble was that he had rewritten
the ballads to suit the taste of his time and had been somewhat disingenuous when challenged to produce the true
text.  The antiquary Ritson, himself not very careful
with texts, denounced Percy as a forger and forcibly gave
it as his opinion that chicanery and falsehood are always
detestable, but never so detestable as when they can be
charged against a cleric of high standing.  This conflict is

only instructive as showing how far both parties were from appreciating the spirit of the ballads, Ritson trying to scholasticize them, and Percy to give them the literary polish of a highly individualistic age.

It must be here explained that the textual method adopted in this book for illustrating the course of the ballad is neither to polish each specimen to suit contemporary taste, nor to rely slavishly on a single variant, but to give a version compressed from several surviving variants when these can be found, and so show the potential completeness that the ballad had while it was still alive.

Perhaps the greatest appreciation of the ballad-proper comes from schoolboys and schoolgirls. It is not only that the simplicity, directness and often the brutality of the narratives please, with absence of the moralizing which they are apt to find insupportable in Wordsworth, a severe handicap to Coleridge and most unfortunate in Shakespeare: but that the communal spirit is strongest in school society, and individualists cannot really appreciate the ballad-proper in its first sense. This last is, I think, what Sir Arthur Quiller-Couch means when he writes in an introduction to his *Oxford Book of Ballads* that the ballad appeals to something childish in the national character. ' Childish ' is not quite the most suitable word, perhaps, because a great number of the ballads he includes refer to experiences beyond the child's understanding; brutal revenge on unfaithful wives, unhappy child-birth, women betrayed and discarded. The much-abused word ' primitive ' may have to serve once more. The ballad-proper seems, then, to have the greatest appeal to members of a closely-bound community, and to those who while experiencing the greater freedom of individualism have no great love of it. So it is no use regretting the decline of the ballad from its first great apple harvest through a ' crab-apple stage ' of broadsheets (Sir Arthur Quiller-Couch's phrase) to its final extinction. The ballad's loss

c

is the gain of the lyric and other individualistic forms. Sir Arthur is of opinion that the ballad cannot be compared with the lyric, as children cannot be compared fairly with grown-up people; but he certainly sets most store by the lyric. And this will, of course, be the opinion of nine out of ten readers of poetry in a modern state, even while making blushing admission, as Sir Philip Sidney did in his *Defence of Poesie*, that the ballad of *Percy and Douglas* (that is, *The Battle of Otterbourne*) moves their heart like a trumpet. But the object of this survey is not to compare one structure of society favourably or unfavourably with another; it is to distinguish their products. Nor is any apology needed for the inclusion of ballads like *Blow the Man Down*, *The Night before Larry was Stretched* or *Wednesbury Cocking*, rough male ballads, but entitled to as much respect as the more sensitive female songs of the *Unquiet Grave* and *Waly, Waly*.

It has already been noted generally that on the strengthening of a cultural centre the old ballads tend to disappear, the epic or prose romance incorporating their substance. There is reason to suppose that the Cuchulain and Finn romances in Ireland, the early books of Livy in Rome, the *Iliad* in Greece, the books of Kings and Judges in Jewish literature, the *Cid* in Spain, the *Chanson Roland* in France, the *Nibelungen Lied* in Germany, all bound up and harmonized a big body of scattered previous balladry. In these and similar compilations there are frequent traces of the intermediate stage of the ballad cycle, of which the English Robin Hood cycle is a convenient example. For the usual succession seems to be, first, the communal ballad, then the bardic ballad, followed by the ballad cycle, the verse romance saga or true epic, finally the prose romance or history. After which the literary epic or poetic drama often appears. Tennyson's *Idylls of the King* are examples of this final literary form; they are based on Malory's prose romance *Morte d'Arthur*. *Morte d'Arthur* is

itself compiled from various verse romances which show
every sign of an earlier history in ballad cycle and bardic
ballad.   But though the ballad proper is often swallowed
up by cultural forms, occasionally fragments of epic and
prose romance are found remodelled in ballad form among
the peoples who live outside the culture or who have
overrun it.

A survey of the ballad in English would be incomplete
without a study of the different national strains that blend
in it.   The Gaelic Celts are now reckoned to have been
among the earliest inhabitants of this country.   The
British Celts did not push these out to Ireland and the
Scottish Highlands so much as absorb them and give them
their own language and culture.   The British Celts in
their turn were not so much pushed out to Wales and
Cornwall as absorbed by the Angles and the Saxons.   The
Danes who settled on the East Coast soon began inter-
marrying with the Anglo-Saxon Celts.   But if we examine
the ancient poetry and romance of the contributory peoples
where these have lived more or less unmixed with each
other, it is surprising to find what absolutely different temperaments they have.   *Beowulf* for the Scandinavians, the
*Nibelungen Lied* for the Teutons, the *Mabinogion* for the
British Celts, *The Cuchulain saga* for the Gaelic Celts, the
*Romaunt of the Rose* for the Norman-French; they seem
continents apart.   The old mediæval theory of the four
humours that compose man may be conveniently used as
an analogy in discussing these various strains.

As warlike peoples they all have the element of fire in
their race, but the Saxon compounds it with earth, the
Gael with air, the Briton with earth and air, the Norse-
man with water, a salty water.   In the English ballad,
where all these strains are in fusion, we get sometimes,
as in the border ballads, even though the subjects are
not usually concerned with the sea, the Norse sea-taste;
sometimes, as in the *Wife of Usher's Well* and *Hugh of*

*Lincoln*, a distinct Gaelic touch; sometimes, as in *Wednesbury Cocking* and *The Old Cloak*, an obstinate Saxon strain. Sometimes there is a curious intertwining of strands, as in *Loving Mad Tom*, where Saxon and Gael dispute possession of Tom's soul; in the *Demon Lover* there is a curious soft Southern stanza in the rude companionship of the Norse, which heightens the poem strangely. The South has made a considerable contribution to the English ballad. For four hundred years, in the Roman occupation, England was ruled from the South. The Norman Conquest made French the official language in England for three hundred years. And until the end of the Middle Ages the fountainhead of the national religion was at Rome. The ballad stanza itself is from the South; it occurs first, it is said, in the camp songs of the Roman Legionaries. It is by this blending of humours that English poetry, ballad, lyric and all, has won its great renown, for where the air and fire of the Gael, the sea and fire of the Norse, the earth and fire of the Saxons can be reconciled in amity with other lesser contributions, that fifth essence or quintessence of poetry appears, which is variously known as the spirit of wonder, as genius, as divine inspiration. It is clear that the communal authorship of the ballad-proper will produce this harmony more often than the individualistic poet. The great scope of Shakespeare, Donne and Keats has been, not unwisely, attributed to the rare power they possessed of reconciling the conflicting temperaments of a mixed English ancestry in verse forms that were largely of Greek, Italian, French and Spanish origin. The prominent poets of a relatively unmixed race usually have in them very few contradictions with which their poetry can make play and enlarge itself, so that there is a tendency to stimulate it by mere technique, which does not make it any better as poetry.

1925.

# BALLADS

# THE MAID FREED FROM THE GALLOWS: OR, THE BRIARY BUSH

A ballad of simple structure: common in variants all over Europe from Finland to Sicily. See Child's *English and Scottish Popular Ballads*.

" Hold your hand, Lord Judge," she says,
  " Yet hold it a little while;
Methinks I see my ain dear father
  Coming wandering many a mile.

" O have you brought me gold, fathér?
  Or have you brought me fee?
Or are you come to save my life
  From off this gallows-tree? "

" I have not brought you gold, daughtér,
  Nor have I brought you fee,
But I am come to see you hangd,
  As you this day shall be."

" O the briary bush, the bush
  That pricks my heart so sore!
For once I am in this briary bush,
  Oh, I shall be free no more! "

The verses run thus until she has seen her mother, her brother, and her sister likewise arrive, and all refuse her ransom, but then:
  " Methinks I see my ain dear lover," etc.

" I have not brought you gold, true-love,
  Nor yet have I brought fee,
But I am come to save thy life
  From off this gallows-tree."

" O the briary bush, the bush
  That pricked my heart so sore!
But now I am out of this briary bush,
  Oh, I shall go in no more!"

" Gae hame, gae hame, my father," she says,
  " Gae hame and saw yer seed;
And I wish not a pickle¹ of it may grow
  But the thistle and the weed.

" Gae hame, gae hame, gae hame, mothér,
  Gae hame and brew yer yill²;
And I wish the girds³ may a' loup⁴ off,
  And the Deil it a' may spill.

" Gae hame, gae hame, gae hame, brothér,
  Gae hame and kiss yer wife;
And I wish that the first news I may hear
  Is that she has tane your life.

" Gae hame, gae hame,  my sister," she says,
  " Gae hame and sew yer seam;
I wish that the needle-point may break,
  And the craws pyke out yer een."

¹ grain.    ² ale.    ³ barrel-hoops.    ⁴ leap.

# THE CLEVELAND LYKE WAKE DIRGE

Another ballad of simple structure from Sir Walter Scott's *Border Minstrelsy;* two verses from Blakeborough's *Wit, Character, Folklore and Customs of the North Riding.* This song continued to be sung over corpses in remote parts of Yorkshire until about 1800. Whinnymuir is an actual moor in the Cleveland district. *Sleet* is probably a corruption of ' *selte*,' i.e. salt, which it was customary to lay in a platter on the breast of the corpse.

> This ae[1] nighte, this ae nighte,
> — *Every nighte and alle ;*
> Fire and sleet and candle-lighte;
> *And Christe receive thy saule.*

> When thou from hence away art past,
> — *Every nighte and alle,*
> To Whinny-muir thou com'st at last;
> *And Christe receive thy saule.*

> If ever thou gavest hosen and shoon
> — *Every nighte and alle,*
> Sit thee down and put them on;
> *And Christe receive thy saule.*

> If hosen and shoon thou ne'er gav'st nane,
> — *Every nighte and alle,*
> The whinnes sall pick thee to the bare bane;
> *And Christe receive thy saule.*

> From Whinny-muir when thou may'st pass,
> — *Every nighte and alle,*
> To Brig[2] o' Dread thou com'st at last;
> *And Christe receive thy saule.*

[1] one.     [2] Bridge.

If ever thou gave of thy silver and gold,
 — *Every nighte and alle,*
At Brig o' Dread thou'lt find foothold;
 *And Christe receive thy saule.*

If silver or gold thou ne'er gavest nane,
 — *Every nighte and alle,*
Thou'lt tumble down towards Hell's flame;
 *And Christe receive thy saule.*

From Brig o' Dread when thou may'st pass,
 — *Every nighte and alle,*
To Purgatory fire thou com'st at last;
 *And Christe receive thy saule.*

If ever thou gavest meat or drink,
 — *Every nighte and alle,*
The fire sall never make thee shrink;
 *And Christe receive thy saule.*

If meat or drink thou ne'er gav'st nane,
 — *Every nighte and alle,*
The fire will burn thee to the bare bane;
 *And Christe receive thy saule.*

This ae nighte, this ae nighte,
 — *Every nighte and alle,*
Fire and sleet and candle-lighte,
 *And Christe receive thy saule.*

# THE FALSE KNIGHT ON THE ROAD

First printed in Motherwell's *Minstrelsy*. There is a Swedish ballad with the same plot in which there is a witch who takes the place of the false knight. The peat was the schoolboys' customary contribution to the schoolroom fire. The implication of the piece is that the devil will carry off the boy if he can nonplus him. These contests of wit are common in early balladry. See *Child*.

" O whare are ye gaun?"
    Quo the fause knicht upon the road:
" I'm gaun to the scule,"
    Quo the wee boy, and still he stude.

" What is that upon your back?" Quo, etc.
" Atweel[1] it is my bukes." Quo, etc.

" What's that ye've got in your arm?"
" Atweel it is my peit."

" Wha's aucht[2] they sheep?"
" They are mine and my mither's."

" How monie o' them are mine?"
" A' they that hae blue tails."

" I wiss ye were on yon tree:"
" And a gude ladder under me."

" And the ladder for to break:"
" And you for to fa down."

" I wiss ye were in yon sie:"
" And a gude bottom under me."

" And the bottom for to break:"
" And ye to be drowned."

[1] Wot well.          [2] Who owns.

43

# THE TWA CORBIES

From Scott's *Minstrelsy of the Scottish Border*. There is an English ballad, *The Three Ravens*, on the same general theme, but in a major key; the hounds, hawks and lady would not leave their master. See *Child*.

As I was walking all alane,
I heard twa corbies[1] making a mane;
The tane unto the t'other say,
"Where sall we gang and dine to-day?"

"In behint yon auld fail[2] dyke
I wot there lies a new slain knight;
And naebody kens that he lies there,
But his hawk, his hound, and lady fair.

"His hound is to the hunting gane,
His hawk to fetch the wild-fowl hame,
His lady's ta'en another mate,
So we may mak our dinner sweet.

"Ye'll sit on his white hause-bane,[3]
And I'll pike out his bonny blue een;
Wi ae lock o' his gowden hair
We'll theek[4] our nest when it grows bare.

"Mony a one for him makes mane,
But nane sall ken where he is gane;
O'er his white banes, when they are bare,
The wind sall blaw for evermair."

[1] crows.    [2] turf.    [3] neckbone.    [4] line.

44

# KEMP OWYNE

From Motherwell's *Minstrelsy*. It is connected with an Icelandic saga, but Kemp—that is, Knight—Owyne is probably an ancient Welsh hero, Owain ap Urien, the King of Reged. See *Child*.

Her mother died when she was young,
    Which gave her cause to make great moan;
Her father married the warst woman
    That ever lived in Christendom.

She servéd her with foot and hand,
    In everything that she could dee,[1]
Till once, in an unlucky time,
    She threw her in ower Craigy's sea.

Says, " Lie you there, dove Isabel,
    And all my sorrows lie with thee;
Till Kemp Owyne come ower the sea,
    And borrow[2] you with kisses three,
Let all the warld do what they will,
    Oh, borrowed shall you never be! "

Her breath grew strang, her hair grew lang,
    And twisted thrice about the tree,
And all the people, far and near,
    Thought that a savage beast was she.

These news did come to Kemp Owyne,
    Where he lived, far beyond the sea;
He hasted him to Craigy's sea,
    And on the savage beast lookd he.

Her breath was strang, her hair was lang,
    And twisted was about the tree,
And with a swing she came about:
    " Come to Craigy's sea, and kiss with me."

---

[1] do.          [2] ransom.

45

" Here is a royal belt," she cried,
 " That I have found in the green sea;
And while your body it is on,
 Drawn shall your blood never be;
But if you touch me, tail or fin,
 I vow my belt your death shall be."


He stepped in, gave her a kiss,
 The royal belt he brought him wi';
Her breath was strang, her hair was lang,
 And twisted twice about the tree,
And with a swing she came about:
 " Come to Craigy's sea, and kiss with me."


" Here is a royal ring," she said,
 " That I have found in the green sea;
And while your finger it is on,
 Drawn shall your blood never be;
But if you touch me, tail or fin,
 I swear my ring your death shall be."


He stepped in, gave her a kiss,
 The royal ring he brought him wi';
Her breath was strang, her hair was lang,
 And twisted ance about the tree,
And with a swing she came about:
 " Come to Craigy's sea, and kiss with me."


" Here is a royal brand," she said,
 " That I have found in the green sea;
And while your body it is on,
 Drawn shall your blood never be;
But if you touch me, tail or fin,
 I swear my brand your death shall be."

He stepped in, gave her a kiss,
   The royal brand he brought him wi';
Her breath was sweet, her hair grew short,
   And twisted nane about the tree,
And smilingly she came about,
   As fair a woman as fair could be.

"O was it wolf into the wood,
   Or was it fish intill the sea,
Or was it man, or wily woman,
   My true love, that misshapit thee?"

"It was na wolf into the wood,
   Nor was it fish intill the sea,
But it was my fause stepmother,
   An wae an weary mot she be.

"O a heavier weird[1] light her upon
Than ever fell on wily woman;
Her hair's grow rough, an her teeth's grow lang,
An on her four feet sal she gang.
Nane sall tack pitty her upon,
But in Wormie's Wood she sall ay won."[2]

      [1] fate.        [2] live.

# SIR PATRICK SPENS

Compressed from the many variants in Professor Child's collection. The ballad is probably founded on events of the reign of Alexander III of Scotland, whose daughter Margaret was married in 1281 to Eric, King of Norway. She was conducted to her husband in August of that year by knights and nobles. Many of these were drowned on the homeward voyage. The daughter of the marriage, to whom the crown of Scotland had fallen in 1286, was affianced in 1290 to the eldest son of our Edward I, but died on the way to England, possibly in a storm off the coast of Scotland: she was known as the "Maid of Norway." This ballad seems to be a confusion of the two stories. Sir Patrick Spens is not a historical figure otherwise than in the ballad.

The King sits in Dumfermlin toun
  Drinking the blude-red wine:
"O, whar will I get a skilly[1] skipper
  Will sail this good ship of mine?"

Then up and spake an eldern knight
  Sat at the King's right knee:
"Sir Patrick Spens is the best sailór
  That ever sailed the sea."

The King has written a braid lettér
  And sealed it with his hand,
And sent it to Sir Patrick Spens
  Was walking on the strand.

"Oh who is the man has done this deed,
  This ill deed done to me?
To send me out this time of the year
  To sail upon the sea?"

---

[1] skilful.

"To Norraway, to Norraway,
    To Norraway o'er the faem.
The King's daughter of Norraway,
    'Tis I must bring her hame."

They have mounted sail on a Monday morn
    With all the haste they may
And they have landed in Norraway
    Upon the Wednesday.

They had not been a week, a week
    In Norraway but three,
Till lords of Norraway gan to say
    "Ye spend all our white monie."

"Ye spend all our good kingis gowd
    But and[1] our queenis fee."[2]
"Ye lie, ye lie, ye liars loud:
    Full loud I hear you lie."[3]

"For I have brought as much white monie
    As will gain[4] my men and me.
I have brought a half-fou[5] of good red gowd
    Out o'er the sea with me."

"Be it wind or weet, be it snow or sleet
    Our ships must sail the morn."
"O ever alack my master dear,
    I fear a deadly storm."

"I saw the new moon late yestreen
    With the old moon in her arm.
And if we go to sea, master,
    I fear a deadly storm."

---

[1] also.        [2] dowry.
[3] These two lines also occur in *The Battle of Otterbourne*, and in many other ballads. The first two lines of the twelfth stanza are also movable property; sometimes substituting "week" for "league," as in stanza 7. Repetition and the use of the number three are among the few characteristic devices of the early ballad. They are most evident in *Kemp Owyne*, but can be found in almost every ballad in the first part of this book.
[4] serve.        [5] half-bushel.

D

They had not sailed a league, a league,
  A league but barely three,
Came wind and weet and snow and sleet
  And gurly[1] grew the sea.

" O where will I get a pretty boy
  Will take my steer in hand
Till I get up to the tall topmast
  To see if I can spy land ? "

He had not gone a step, a step,
  A step but barely ane,
When a bolt flew out of the gude ship's side,
  And the salt sea it came in.

They fetch a web of the silken cloth,
  Another of the twine.
They wapped[2] them round the gude ship's side,
  But still the sea came in.

Laeth, laeth, were our Scottish lords
  To wet their cork-heeled shoon,
But yet ere all the play was played
  Their hats were wet aboon.[3]

O lang, lang may their ladies sit
  With their fans into their hand,
Or ever they see Sir Patrick Spens
  Come sailing to the land.

O lang lang may the ladies stand
  With their gold kaims in their hair
Waiting for their own dear lords
  That they shall not see mair.

---

[1] rough.      [2] swathed.      [3] above.

Half ower, half ower to Aberdour
  It is fifty fathoms deep,
And there lies good Sir Patrick Spens
  With the Scots lords at his feet.

# THE WIFE OF USHER'S WELL

From Scott's *Minstrelsy of the Scottish Border.* In other
versions Jesus Christ sends the sons back for a night in answer
to prayer. See *Child.*

There lived a wife[1] at Usher's Well,
 And a wealthy wife was she;
She had three stout and stalwart sons
 And sent them o'er the sea.

They hadna been a week from her,
 A week but barely ane,
Whan word came to the carlin[2] wife
 That her three sons were gane.

They hadna been a week from her,
 A week but barely three,
Whan word came to the carlin wife
 That her sons she'd never see.

"I wish the wind may never cease,
 Nor fashes[3] in the flood,
Till my three sons come hame to me,
 In earthly flesh and blood."

It fell about the Martinmass,
 When nights are lang and mirk,
The carlin wife's three sons came hame,
 And their hats were o' the birk.[4]

It neither grew in dyke nor ditch,
 Nor yet in ony sheugh[5];
But at the gates o' Paradise,
 That birk grew fair eneugh.

  .  .  .  .

[1] woman.  [2] old woman.  [3] troubles.
[4] birch.  [5] ditch or furrow.

" Blow up the fire, my maidens,
   Bring water from the well;
For a' my house shall feast this night,
   Since my three sons are well."

And she has made to them a bed,
   She's made it large and wide,
And she's taen her mantle her about,
   Sat down at the bed-side.

    .    .    .    .    .

Up then crew the red, red cock,
   And up and crew the gray;
The eldest to the youngest said,
   'Tis time we were away.

The cock he hadna crawd but once,
   And clappd his wings at a',
When the youngest to the eldest said,
   Brother, we must awa.

"The cock doth craw, the day doth daw[1]:
   The channerin'[2] worm doth chide;
Gin we be mist out o' our place,
   A sair pain we maun bide.

"Fare ye weel, my mother dear!
   Fareweel to barn and byre!
And fare ye weel, the bonny lass
   That kindles my mother's fire!"

       [1] dawn.            [2] petulant.

# GRAEME AND BEWICK

From Scott's *Minstrelsy*. Scott remarks that this ballad is remarkable as containing one of the latest allusions to the practice of brotherhood in arms. See *Child*.

Gude Lord Graeme is to Carlisle gane,
    Sir Robert Bewick there met he,
And arm in arm to the wine they did go,
    And they drank till they were baith merry

Gude Lord Graeme has ta'en up the cup,
    "Sir Robert Bewick, and here's to thee!
And here's to our twa sons at hame!
    For they like us best in our ain country."—

"O were your son a lad like mine,
    And learn'd some books that he could read,
They might hae been twa brethren bold,
    And they might hae bragged[1] the Border side.

"But your son's a lad, and he is but bad,
    And billy[2] to my son he canna be;"

    .    .    .    .    .    .

"I sent him to the schools, and he wadna learn;
    I bought him books, and he wadna read;
But my blessing shall he never earn,
    Till I see how his arm can defend his head."—

Gude Lord Graeme has a reckoning call'd,
    A reckoning then calléd he;
And he paid a crown, and it went roun',
    It was all for the gude wine and free.

[1] defied.
[2] billy is the same word as "bully," which in English has lost its original sense of "friend" and come to mean "hearty fellow," and finally "tyrant."

And he has to the stable gane,
　　Where there stood thirty steeds and three;
He's ta'en his ain horse amang them a',
　　And hame he rade sae manfully.

"Welcome, my auld father!" said Christie Graeme,
　　" But where sae lang frae hame were ye ? "—
" It's I hae been at Carlisle town,
　　And a baffled[1] man by thee I be.

" I hae been at Carlisle town,
　　Where Sir Robert Bewick he met me;
He says ye're a lad, and ye are but bad,
　　And billy to his son ye canna be.

" I sent ye to the schools, and ye wadna learn;
　　I bought ye books, and ye wadna read;
Therefore my blessing ye shall never earn,
　　Till I see with Bewick thou save my head."[2]

" Now, God forbid, my auld father,
　　That ever sic a thing should be!
Billy Bewick was my master, and I was his scholar,
　　And aye sae weel as he learnéd me."

" O hold thy tongue, thou limmer loon,[3]
　　And of thy talking let me be!
If thou does na end me this quarrel soon,
　　There is my glove, I'll fight wi' thee."

Then Christie Graeme he stoopéd low
　　Unto the ground, you shall understand;—
" O father, put on your glove again,
　　The wind has blown it from your hand."

___

[1] disgraced.　　[2] a variant of " save my face."　　[3] rascal, lout,

" What's that thou says, thou limmer loon ?
   How dares thou stand to speak to me ?
If thou does na end this quarrel soon,
   There's my right hand, thou shalt fight with me."

Then Christie Graeme's to his chamber gane,
   To consider weel what then should be;
Whether he should fight with his auld fathér,
   Or with his billy Bewick, he.

" If I should kill my billy dear,
   God's blessing I shall never win;
But if I strike at my auld father,
   I think 'twould be a mortal sin.

" But if I kill my billy dear,
   It is God's will, so let it be;
But I make a vow, ere I gang frae hame,
   That I shall be the next man die."—

Then he's put on's back a gude auld jack,[1]
   And on his head a cap of steel,
And sword and buckler by his side;
   O gin[2] he did not become them weel!

We'll leave off talking of Christie Graeme,
   And talk of him again belive[3];
And we will talk of bonny Bewick,
   Where he was teaching his scholars five.

When he had taught them well to fence,
   And handle swords without any doubt,
He took his sword under his arm,
   And he walk'd his father's close about.

_____

[1] coat cf mail.          [2] if.          [3] soon.

He look'd atween him and the sun,
  And a' to see what there might be,
Till he spied a man in armour bright,
  Was riding that way most hastily.


" O wha is yon, that came this way,
  Sae hastily that hither came ?
I think it be my brother dear,
  I think it be young Christie Graeme.


" Ye're welcome here, my billy dear,
  And thrice ye're welcome unto me ! "—
" But I'm wae to say, I've seen the day,
  When I am come to fight wi' thee.


" My father's gane to Carlisle town,
  Wi' your father Bewick there met he:
He says I'm a lad, and I am but bad,
  And a baffled man I trow I be.


" He sent me to schools, and I wadna learn;
  He bought me books, and I wadna read;
Sae my father's blessing I'll never earn,
  Till he see how my arm can guard my head."


" O God forbid, my billy dear,
  That ever such a thing should be !
We'll take three men on either side,
  And see if we can our fathers agree."


" O hold thy tongue, now, billy Bewick,
  And of thy talking let me be !
But if thou'rt a man, as I'm sure thou art,
  Come o'er the dyke, and fight wi' me."

" But I hae nae harness, billy, on my back,
   As weel I see is now on thine."—
" But as little harness as is on thy back,
   As little, billy, shall be on mine."—

Then he's thrown off his coat o' mail,
   His cap of steel away flung he;
He stuck his spear into the ground,
   And he tied his horse unto a tree.

Then Bewick has thrown off his cloak,
   And's psalter-book frae's hand flung he;
He laid his hand upon the dyke,
   And ower he lap most manfully.

O they hae fought for twa lang hours;
   When twa long hours were come and gane,
The sweat drapp'd fast frae off them baith,
   But a drap of blude could not be seen.

Till Graeme gae Bewick an awkward stroke,
   Ane awkward stroke strucken sickerly[1];
He has hit him under the left breast,
   And dead-wounded to the ground fell he.

" Rise up, rise up, now, billy dear,
   Arise and speak three words to me!
Whether thou's gotten thy deadly wound,
   Or if God and good leeching may succour thee ? "

" O horse, O horse, now, billy Graeme,
   And get thee far from hence with speed;
And get thee out of this countrie,
   That none may know who has done the deed."—

[1] surely.

" O I have slain thee, billy Bewick,
    If this be true thou tellest to me;
But I made a vow, ere I came frae hame,
    That aye the next man I wad be."

He has pitch'd his sword in a moodie-hill,[1]
    And he has leap'd twenty lang feet and three,
And on his ain sword's point he lap,
    And dead upon the ground fell he.

'Twas then came up Sir Robert Bewick,
    And his brave son alive saw he;
" Rise up, rise up, my son," he said,
    " For I think ye hae gotten the victory."

" O hold your tongue, my father dear,
    Of your prideful talking let me be!
Ye might hae drunken your wine in peace,
    And let me and my billy be.

" Gae dig a grave, baith wide and deep,
    And a grave to hold baith him and me;
But lay Christie Graeme on the sunny side,
    For I'm sure he won the victory."

" Alack! a wae!" auld Bewick cried,
    " Alack! was I not much to blame?
I'm sure I've lost the liveliest lad
    That e'er was born unto my name."

" Alack! a wae!" quo' gude Lord Graeme,
    " I'm sure I hae lost the deeper lack[2]!
I durst hae ridden the Border through,
    Had Christie Graeme been at my back.

1 mole-hill.                    2 loss.

" Had I been led through Liddesdale,
    And thirty horsemen guarding me,
And Christie Graeme been at my back,
    Sae soon as he had set me free!

" I've lost my hopes, I've lost my joy,
    I've lost the key but and the lock;
I durst hae ridden the world round,
    Had Christie Graeme been at my back."

# THE DEMON LOVER

Sometimes called *James Harris*. In other versions, of which there are several, we learn that the woman was named Jane Reynolds. James Harris, to whom she had plighted her troth years before, seduced her from her husband, a carpenter: or rather the Fiend in her old lover's likeness did so. This version is from Scott's *Minstrelsy*. See *Child*.

"O where have you been, my long, long love,
    This long seven years and more?"—
"O I'm come to seek my former vows
    Ye granted me before."—

"O hold your tongue of your former vows,
    For they will breed sad strife;
O hold your tongue of your former vows,
    For I am become a wife."

He turn'd him right and round about,
    And the tear blinded his ee;
"I wad never hae trodden on Irish ground,
    If it had not been for thee.

"I might hae had a king's daughtér,
    Far, far beyond the sea;
I might have had a king's daughtér,
    Had it not been for love o' thee."—

"If ye might have had a king's daughtér,
    Yoursel' ye had to blame;
Ye might have taken the king's daughtér,
    For ye kenned that I was nane.

"If I was to leave my husband dear,
    And my two babes also,
O what have you to take me to,
    If with you I should go?"—

" I hae seven ships upon the sea,
　　The eighth brought me to land;
With four and twenty bold mariners,
　　And music on every hand."

She has taken up her two little babes,
　　Kiss'd them baith cheek and chin;
" O fair ye weel, my ain two babes,
　　For I'll never see you again."

She set her foot upon the ship,
　　No mariners could she behold;
But the sails were o' the taffety,
　　And the masts o' the beaten gold.

She had not sail'd a league, a league,
　　A league but barely three,
When dismal grew his countenance,
　　And drumlie[1] grew his ee.

They had not sailed a league, a league,
　　A league but barely three,
Until she espied his cloven foot,
　　And she wept right bitterly.

" O hold your tongue of your weeping," says he,
　　" Of your weeping now let me be;
I will show you how the lilies grow
　　On the banks of Italy."—

" O what hills are yon, yon pleasant hills,
　　That the sun shines sweetly on ?"—
" O yon are the hills of heaven," he said,
　　" Where you will never won."—

[1] gloomy.

" O whaten a mountain is yon," she said,
  " All so dreary wi' frost and snow ? "
" O yon is the mountain of hell," he cried,
  " Where you and I will go."

He strack the tap-mast wi' his hand,
  The fore-mast wi' his knee;
And he brake that gallant ship in twain,
  And sank her in the sea.

# THE BATTLE OF OTTERBOURNE

Otherwise known as *Chevy Chace*, or *Percy and Douglas*.
This version is from Scott's *Minstrelsy*. It is an incident in the
raid into England undertaken in revenge of the invasion of
Scotland by Richard II in 1387. There is a more detailed if
less poetical English version in Percy's *Reliques*, in which,
naturally, the raid is made into Scotland, and Lord Percy is slain,
not captured. The Scottish version is the earliest. See *Child*

It fell about the Lammas tide,
　　When the muir[1]-men win[2] their hay,
The doughty Douglas bound him to ride
　　Into England, to drive a prey.

He chose the Gordons and the Graemes,
　　With them the Lindsays, light and gay;
But the Jardines wad not with him ride,
　　And they rue it to this day.

And he has burn'd the dales of Tyne,
　　And part of Bambroughshire;
And three good towers on Reidswire fells,
　　He left them all on fire.

And he march'd up to Newcastéll,
　　And rode it round about;
" O wha's the lord of this castéll,
　　O wha's the lady o't ? "

But up spake proud Lord Percy then,
　　And O but he spake high!
" I am the lord of this castéll,
　　My wife's the lady gay."

<hr>

¹ moor.　　　² make.

" If thou'rt the lord of this castéll,
    Sae weel it pleases me!
For ere I cross the Border fells,
    The tane[1] of us shall die."

He took a lang spear in his hand,
    Shod with the metal free,[2]
And for to meet the Douglas there,
    He rode right furiously.

But O how pale his lady look'd,
    Frae aff the castle wa',
When down before the Scottish spear
    She saw proud Percy fa'.

" Had we twa been upon the green,
    And never an eye to see,
I wad hae had you, flesh and fell;[3]
    But your sword sall gae wi' me."

" But gae ye up to Otterbourne,
    And wait there dayés three,
And if I come not ere three dayés end,
    A fause knight ca' ye me."

" The Otterbourne's a bonnie burn;
    'Tis pleasant there to be;
But there is nought at Otterbourne,
    To feed my men and me.

" The deer rins wild on hill and dale.
    The birds fly wild from tree to tree;
But there is neither bread nor kale,[4]
    To fend[5] my men and me.

[1] one of two.    [2] precious.    [3] skin.
[4] broth made from herbs.    [5] keep, support.

"Yet I will stay at Otterbourne,
  Where you shall welcome be;
And if ye come not at three days' end,
  A fause lord I'll ca' thee."

"Thither will I come," proud Percy said,
  "By the might of Our Lady!"
"There will I bide thee," said the Douglas,
  "My troth I plight to thee."

They lighted high on Otterbourne,
  Upon the bent[1] sae brown;
They lighted high on Otterbourne,
  And threw their pallions[2] down.

And he that had a bonnie boy,
  Sent out his horse to grass;
And he that had not a bonnie boy,
  His ain servant he was.

But up then spake a little page,
  Before the peep of dawn—
"O waken ye, waken ye, my good lord,
  For Percy's hard at hand."

"Ye lie, ye lie, ye liar loud!
  Sae loud I hear ye lie:
For Percy had not men yestreen
  To fight my men and me.

"But I have dream'd a dreary dream,
  Beyond the Isle of Sky;
I saw a dead man win a fight,
  And I think that man was I."

[1] field.    [2] pavilions, tents.

He belted on his guid braid sword,
   And to the field he ran;
But he forgot the helmet good,
   That should have kept his brain.

When Percy wi' the Douglas met,
   I wat he was fu' fain;
They swakked[1] their swords, till sair they swat,
   And the blood ran down like rain.

But Percy with his guid braid sword,
   That could so sharply wound,
Has wounded Douglas on the brow,
   Till he fell to the ground.

Then he called on his little foot-page,
   And said—" Run speedily,
And fetch my ain dear sister's son,
   Sir Hugh Montgomery.

" My nephew good," the Douglas said,
   " What recks the death of ane!
Last night I dream'd a dreary dream,
   And I ken the day's thy ain.

" My wound is deep; I fain would sleep;
   Take thou the vanguard of the three,
And hide me by the bracken bush,
   That grows on yonder lily lea.

" O bury me by the bracken bush,
   Beneath the blooming brere,
Let never living mortal ken
   That ere a kindly Scot lies here."

[1] smote together.

He lifted up that noble lord,
    Wi' the saut tear in his ee;
He hid him in the bracken bush,
    That his merry-men might not see.

The moon was clear, the day drew near,
    The spears in flinders[1] flew,
But mony a gallant Englishman
    Ere day the Scotsmen slew.

The Gordons good in English blood
    They steeped their hose and shoon;
The Lindsays flew like fire about,
    Till all the fray was done.

The Percy and Montgomery met,
    That either of other were fain[2];
They swakkéd swords, and they twa' swat,
    And aye the blood ran down between.

" Now yield thee, yield thee, Percy," he said,
    " Or else I vow I'll lay thee low! "
" To whom must I yield," quoth Earl Percy,
    " Now that I see it must be so? "

" Thou shalt not yield to lord nor loon,
    Nor yet shalt thou yield to me;
But yield thee to the bracken bush,
    That grows upon yon lily lea."

" I will not yield to a bracken bush,
    Nor yet will I yield to a brere;
But I would yield to Earl Douglas,
    Or Sir Hugh the Montgomery, if he were here."

---

[1] fragments.      [2] glad.

As soon as he knew it was Montgomery,
   He struck his sword's point in the ground;
The Montgomery was a courteous knight,
   And quickly took him by the hand.

This deed was done at the Otterbourne,
   About the breaking of the day;
Earl Douglas was buried at the bracken bush,
   And the Percy led captive away.

# JOHNNY COCK

Sent to Percy by a lady of Carlisle in 1780. It is the fullest
of many versions, but the references to American leather and
to bows bought in London imply a late recasting. See *Child*.

Johny he has risen up i' the morn,
 Calls for water to wash his hands;
But little knew he that his bloody hounds
 Were bound in iron bands,
 Were bound in iron bands.[1]

Johny's mother has gotten word o' that,
 And care-bed[2] she has taen:
" O Johny, for my benison,
 I beg you'll stay at hame;
For the wine so red, and the well baken bread,
 My Johny shall want nane.

" There are seven forsters at Pickeram Side,
 At Pickeram where they dwell,
And for a drop of thy heart's bluid
 They wad ride the fords of hell."

Johny he's gotten word of that,
 And he's turnd wondrous keen;
He's put off the red scarlett,
 And he's put on the Lincolm green.

With a sheaf of arrows by his side,
 And a bent bow in his hand,
He's mounted on a prancing steed,
 And he has ridden fast oer the strand.

[1] The sense of this is probably that his mother had imprisoned Johny's
hounds to deter him from the chase : but the verse may be corrupt.
[2] almost (or quite) sick-bed.

He's up i' Braidhouplee, and down i' Bradyslee,
    And under a buss[1] o' broom,
And there he found a good dun deer,
    Feeding in a buss of ling.

Johny shot, and the dun deer lap,[2]
    And she lap wondrous wide,
Until they came to the wan water,
    And he stemd[3] her of her pride.

He has taen out the little pen-knife,
    'Twas full three quarters[4] long,
And he has taen out of that dun deer
    The liver but and the tongue.

They eat of the flesh, and they drank of the blood,
    And the blood it was so sweet,
Which cause Johný and his bloody hounds,
    To fall in a deep sleep.

By then came an old palmér,
    And an ill death may he die!
For he's away to Pickram Side,
    As fast as he can drie.[5]

" What news, what news ? " says the Seven Forsters,
    " What news have ye brought to me ? "
" I have noe news," the palmer said,
    " But what I saw with my eye.

" High up i' Braidhouplee, low down i' Bradyslee,
    And under a buss of scroggs,[6]
O there I spied a well-wight[7] man,
    Sleeping among his dogs.

---

[1] bush.    [2] leaped.    [3] ended.    [4] This measure is obscure.
    [5] manage.    [6] stunted bushes.    [7] bold or sturdy.

" His coat it was of light Lincólm,
 And his breeches of the same,
His shoes of the American leather,
 And gold buckles tying them."

Up bespake the Seven Forsters,
 Up bespake they ane and a':
O that is Johny o' Cockleys Well,
 And near him we will draw.

O the first stroke that they gave him,
 They struck him by the knee;
Then up bespake his sister's son:
 " O the next'll gar[1] him die! "

" O some they count ye well-wight men,
 But I do count ye nane;
For you might well ha wakend me,
 And askd gin I wad be taen.

" The wildest wolf in a' this wood
 Wad not ha done so by me;
She'd ha wet her foot i' the wan watér,
 And sprinkled it oer my brae,[2]
And if that wad not ha wakend me,
 She wad ha gone and let me be.

" O bows of yew, if ye be true,
 In London, where ye were bought,
Fingers five, get up belive,
 Manhuid shall fail me nought."

He has killd the Seven Forsters,
 He has killd them all but ane,
And that won scarce to Pickeram Side,
 To carry the bode-words[3] hame.

---

[1] make.   [2] brow.   [3] fatal news.

" Is there never a boy in a' this wood
   That will tell what I can say;
That will go for me to Cockleys Well,
   Tell my mither to fetch me away ? "

There was a boy into that wood,
   That carried the tidings away,
And many ae was the well-wight man
   At the fetching o' Johny away.

# THE CHERRY TREE CAROL

This highly popular carol is founded on a story in the Pseudo-Matthew's Gospel, Chapter XX. See *Child*.

Joseph was an old man
And an old man was he
When he married Mary
The Queen of Galilee.

Joseph and Mary walkéd
Through an orchard green,
Where was berries and cherries
As thick as might be seen.

O then bespoke Mary
So meek and so mild,
" Pluck me a cherry, Joseph,
For I am with child."

O then bespoke Joseph
With words most unkind,
" Let him pluck thee cherries
That got thee with child."

O then bespoke the Babe
Within his mother's womb,
" Bow down then the tallest tree
For my mother to have some."

Then bowed down the tallest tree
Unto his mother's hand,
Then she cried, " See, Joseph,
I have cherries at command."

As Joseph was a walking
  He heard angels sing,
" This night shall be born
  Our heavenly king."

He neither shall be born
  In house nor in hall,
Nor in the place of Paradise,
  But in an ox's stall.

He neither shall be clothéd
  In purple nor in pall
But all in fair linen
  As wear babies all.

He neither shall be rockéd
  In silver nor in gold
But in a wooden cradle
  That rocks on the mould.

Then Mary took her babe
  And sat him on her knee:
" I pray thee now, dear child,
  Tell how this world shall be."

" O I shall be as dead, Mother,
  As the stones in the wall:
O the stones in the street, Mother,
  Shall mourn for me all.

" Upon Easter Day, Mother,
  My rising shall be:
Oh, the sun and the moon
  Shall uprise with me."

# HUGH OF LINCOLN

Child quotes twenty-one versions of this ballad: this is from Jamieson's *Popular Ballads*. In the year 1255 a boy of Lincoln named Hugh was supposed to have been crucified by the Jews in contempt of Christ after various tortures: for which crime eighteen Jews were hanged. It is commonly and quite groundlessly charged against the Jews that such murders are done to get blood for the Paschal sacrifice: a charge frequent in Russia under the old regime. Another English boy-saint supposed to have been similarly martyred in 1144 was William of Norwich. Compare Chaucer's *Prioress's Tale*.

Four and twenty bonny boys
    Were playing at the ba',
And by it came him sweet Sir Hugh,
    And he play'd o'er them a'.

He kicked the ba' with his right foot,
    And catch'd it wi' his knee,
And throuch-and-thro' the Jew's window
    He gar'd the bonny ba' flee.

He's done him[1] to the Jew's castell,
    And walkd it round about;
And there he saw the Jew's daughtér,
    At the window looking out.

"Throw down the ba', ye Jew's daughtér,
    Throw down the ba' to me!"
"Never a bit," says the Jew's daughtér,
    "Till up to me come ye."

"How will I come up? How can I come up?
    How can I come to thee?
For as ye did to my auld father,
    The same ye'll do to me."

[1] gone.

76

She's gane till her father's garden,
    And pu'd an apple red and green;
'Twas a' to wyle him, sweet Sir Hugh,
    And to entice him in.

She's led him in through ae dark door,
    And sae has she thro nine;
She's laid him on a dressing-table,
    And stickit him like a swine.

And first came out the thick, thick blood,
    And syne[1] came out the thin,
And syne came out the bonny heart's blood;
    There was nae mair within.

She's row'd[2] him in a cake o' lead,
    Bade him lie still and sleep;
She's thrown him in Our Lady's draw-well,
    Was fifty fathom deep.

When bells were rung, and mass was sung,
    And a' the bairns came hame,
When every lady gat hame her son,
    The Lady Maisry gat nane.

She's ta'en her mantle her about,
    Her coffer by the hand,
And she's gane out to seek her son,
    And wander'd o'er the land.

She's done her to the Jew's castell,
    Where a' were fast asleep:
" Gin ye be there, my sweet Sir Hugh,
    I pray you to me speak."

       [1] next.        [2] rolled or wrapped.

She's done her to the Jew's garden,
    Thought he had been gathering fruit:
" Gin ye be there my sweet Sir Hugh,
    I pray you to me bruit."[1]

She's near'd Our Lady's deep draw-well,
    Was fifty fathom deep:
" Whare'er ye be, my sweet Sir Hugh,
    I pray you to me speak."

" Gae hame, gae hame, my mither dear,
    Prepare my winding sheet,
And at the back o' merry Lincoln
    The morn[2] I will you meet."

Now Lady Maisry is gane hame,
    Made him a winding sheet,
And at the back o' merry Lincoln
    The dead corpse did her meet.

And a' the bells o' merry Lincoln
    Without men's hands were rung,
And a' the books o' merry Lincoln
    Were read without man's tongue,
And ne'er was such a burial
    Sin Adam's days begun.

[1] make a noise.    [2] to-morrow.

# BRUTON TOWN

One of the few early ballads to escape the notice of Professor
Child. It is apparently the same story as that of *Isabella and
the Pot of Basil* which Boccaccio relates in prose and which
Keats made into a poem. But it breaks off short. It is a question
whether Boccaccio's tale and this ballad are drawn from a
common source or whether *Bruton Town* is a rare instance of
an English popular ballad with a literary parentage other than
a Biblical one. For variants and correspondence see *Journal of
English Folk Song Society*, Vol. 2, p. 42, and Vol. 5, pp. 123–
127. The Italian story gives Messina as the scene of the tragedy,
and ennobles the family.

In Bruton Town there lived a farmer
 Who had two sons and one daughter dear:
By day and night they were contriving
 To fill their parent's hearts with fear.

One told his secret to none other
 But unto his brother this he said,
" I think our servant courts our sister,
 I fear they have a mind to wed."

" If he our servant courts our sister,
 That maid from such a shame I'll save:
I'll put an end to all their courtship,
 I'll send him silent to his grave."

A day of hunting was prepared
 In thorny woods where briars grew,
There they did then that young man murder
 And in the brook his body threw.

" Now welcome home, my dear young brothers!
 Our servant man is he behind?"
" We left him where we have been hunting,
 We left him where no man may find."

To bed she went then, crying and lamenting
    Lamenting for her heart's delight.
She slept, she dreamed, she saw him by her
    All bloody-red in piteous plight.

His lovely curls were wet with water
    His body all a-gape with blows.
" O love for thee I suffer murder,
    For thee I lie where no man knows."

She rose up early the morrow morning
    Unto the forest brake she rode,
And there she found her own dear jewel
    All dabbled o'er in a gore of blood.

Dabbled o'er both with blood and water,
    And thus she did her true-love find,
She drew a kerchief from her pocket
    And wiped his eyes though they were blind.

# ROBIN HOOD AND THE THREE SQUIRES

There are at least fifty different ballads commemorating the deeds of Robin Hood, each of these in many variants. See *Child*. He was certainly, in the first place, a real outlaw and flourished in the reign of Richard I, but the growth of legend has obscured the rest of his history. In a sermon preached to Edward VI, Bishop Latimer complains that " I came once myself to a place riding on a journey homeward from London and I sent word overnight into the town that I would preach there in the morning, because it was a holy day, and methought it was a holy day's work: the church stood in my way, and I took my horse and my company and went thither. I thought I should have found a great company in the church, and when I came there the church door was fast locked. I tarried there half an hour and more, and at last the key was found. And one of the parish comes to me and says, ' Sir, this is a busy day with us ; we cannot hear you. It is Robin Hood's Day. The Parish are gone abroad for Robin Hood, I pray you hinder them not.' I was fain there to give place to Robin Hood. It is no laughing matter, my friends, it is a weeping matter, a heavy matter under the pretence for gathering for Robin Hood, a traitor and a thief, to put out a preacher, to prefer Robin Hood before the ministration of God's word."

There are twelve months in all the year,
    As I hear many men say,
But the merriest month in all the year
    Is the merry month of May.

Now Robin Hood is to Nottingham gone,
    With a link-a-down and a-day,
And there he met a silly[1] old woman,
    Was weeping on the way.

" What news ? what news, thou silly old woman ?
    What news hast thou for me ? "
Said she, " There's three squires in Nottingham town
    To-day is condemned to die."

[1] simple.

"O have they parishes burnt?" he said,
  "Or have they ministers slain?
Or have they robbéd any virgin,
  Or with other men's wives have lain?"

"They have no parishes burnt, good sir,
  Nor yet have ministers slain,
Nor have they robbed any virgin,
  Nor with other men's wives have lain."

"O what have they done?" said bold Robin Hood,
  "I pray thee tell to me:"
"It's for slaying of the king's fallow deer,
  Bearing their long bows with thee."

"Dost thou not mind, old woman," he said,
  "Since thou made me sup and dine?
By the truth of my body," quoth bold Robin Hood,
  "You could not tell it in better time."

Now Robin Hood is to Nottingham gone,
  With a link-a-down and a-day,
And there he met with a silly old palmer,
  Was walking along the highway.

"What news? what news, thou silly old man?
  What news, I do thee pray?"
Said he, "Three squires in Nottingham town
  Are condemned to die this day."

"Come change thy apparel with me, old man,
  Come change thy apparel for mine;
Here is forty shillings in good silvér,
  Go drink it in beer or wine."

" O thine apparel is good," he said,
  " And mine is ragged and torn;
Wherever you go, wherever you ride,
  Laugh ne'er an old man to scorn."

" Come change thy apparel with me, old churl,
  Come change thy apparel with mine;
Here are twenty pieces of good broad gold,
  Go feast thy brethren with wine."

Then he put on the old man's hat,
  It stood full high on the crown:
" The first bold bargain that I come at,
  It shall make thee come down."

Then he put on the old man's cloak,
  Was patchd black, blue and red;
He thought no shame all the day long
  To wear the bags of bread.

Then he put on the old man's breeks,
  Was patchd from side to side;
" By the truth of my body," bold Robin gan say,
  " This man lov'd little pride."

Then he put on the old man's hose,
  Were patchd from knee to wrist;
" By the truth of my body," said bold Robin Hood,
  " I'd laugh if I had any list."[1]

Then he put on the old man's shoes,
  Were patchd both beneath and aboon;
Then Robin Hood swore a solemn oath,
  " It's good habit that makes a man."

[1] wish.

Now Robin Hood is to Nottingham gone,
  With a link-a-down and a-down,
And there he met with the proud sheriff,
  Was walking along the town.

" O save, O save, O sheriff," he said,
  " O save, and you may see!
And what will you give to a silly old man
  To-day will your hangman be ? "

" Some suits, some suits," the sheriff he said,
  " Some suits I'll give to thee;
Some suits, some suits, and pence thirteen
  To-day's a hangman's fee."

Then Robin he turns him round about,
  And jumps from stock to stone;
" By the truth of my body," the sheriff he said,
  " That's well jumpt, thou nimble old man."

" I was ne'er a hangman in all my life,
  Nor yet intend to trade;
But curst be he," said bold Robin,
  " That first a hangman was made.

" I've a bag for meal, and a bag for malt,
  And a bag for barley and corn;
A bag for bread, and a bag for beef,
  And a bag for my little small horn.

" I have a horn in my pockét,
  I got it from Robin Hood,
And still when I set it to my mouth,
  For thee it blows little good."

" O wind thy horn, thou proud fellów,
  Of thee I have no doubt;
I wish that thou give such a blast
  Till both thy eyes fall out."

The first loud blast that he did blow,
  He blew both loud and shrill;
A hundred and fifty of Robin Hood's men
  Came riding over the hill.

The next loud blast that he did give,
  He blew both loud and amain,
And quickly sixty of Robin Hood's men
  Came shining over the plain.

" O who are yon," the sheriff he said,
  " Come tripping over the lea? "
" They're my attendants," brave Robin did say,
  " They'll pay a visit to thee."

They took the gallows from the slack,[1]
  They set it in the glen,
They hangd the proud sheriff on that,
  Releasd their own three men.

[1] pass between two hills.

# THE OLD CLOAK

First printed in Ramsay's *Tea Table Miscellany*, 1724, but probably dating from the late sixteenth century. The first part of the seventh stanza is quoted by Shakespeare in *Othello*.

### I

This winter's weather it waxeth cold,
    And frost it freezeth on every hill,
And Boreas blows his blast so bold
    That all our kine he is like to kill.
Bell, my wife, she loves no strife;
    She said unto me quietlye,
" Rise up, and save cow Crumbock's life.
    Man, put thine old cloak about thee ! "

### II

*He.* O Bell, my wife, why dost thou flyte ?[1]
    Thou kens my cloak is very thin:
It is so bare and over worn,
    A crickè[2] thereon cannot renn.
Then I'll no longer borrow nor lend;
    For once I'll new apparell'd be;
To-morrow I'll to town and spend;
    For I'll have a new cloak about me.

### III

*She.* Cow Crumbock is a very good cow:
    She has been always true to the pail;
She has help'd us to butter and cheese, I trow,
    And other things she will not fail.
I would be loth to see her pine.
    Good husband, counsel take of me:
It is not for us to go so fine—
    Man, take thine old cloak about thee !

[1] scold.      [2] cricket.

IV

*He.* My cloak it was a very good cloak,
 It hath been always true to the wear;
But now it is not worth a groat:
 I have had it four and forty year.
Sometime it was of cloth in grain[1]:
 'Tis now but a sigh clout,[2] as you may see:
It will neither hold out wind nor rain;
 And I'll have a new cloak about me.

V

*She.* It is four and forty years ago
 Since the one of us the other did ken;
And we have had, betwixt us two,
 Of children either nine or ten:
We have brought them up to women and men:
 In the fear of God I trow they be:
And why wilt thou thyself misken[3]?
 Man, take thine old cloak about thee!

VI

*He.* O Bell, my wife, why dost thou flyte?
 Now is now, and then was then:
Seek now all the world throughout,
 Thou kens not clowns from gentlemen:
They are clad in black, green, yellow and blue,
 So far above their own degree.
Once in my life I'll take a view;
 For I'll have a new cloak about me.

VII

*She.* King Stephen was a worthy peer;
 His breeches cost him but a crown;
He held them sixpence all too dear,
 Therefore he called the tailor 'lown.'

---

[1] scarlet cloth.    [2] a rag for straining.    [3] mistake.

He was a king and wore the crown,
And thou's but of a low degree:
It's pride that puts this country down:
Man, take thy old cloak about thee!

VIII

*He.* Bell my wife, she loves not strife,
Yet she will lead me, if she can:
And to maintain an easy life
I oft must yield, though I'm good-man.
It's not for a man with a woman to threap,[1]
Unless he first give o'er the plea[2]:
As we began, so will we keep,
And I'll take my old cloak about me.

[1] argue.          [2] resign his point.

# WEDNESBURY COCKING

This ballad is printed in Samuel Butler's *Alps and Sanctuaries:*
he knew it from tradition only, and I cannot find it recorded
elsewhere. The date is probably the end of the eighteenth
century.

At Wednesbury there was a cocking,
    A match between Newton and Scroggins;
The colliers and nailers left work,
    And all to old Spittle's went jogging.
To see this noble sport,
    Many noblemen resorted;
And though they'd but little money,
    Yet that little they freely sported.

There was Jeffery and Colborn from Hampton,
    And Dusty from Bilston was there;
Flummery he came from Darlaston,
    And he was as rude as a bear.
There was old Will from Walsall,
    And Smacker from Westbromwich come;
Blind Robin he came from Rowley,
    And staggering he went home.

Ralph Moody came hobbling along,
    As though he some cripple was mocking,
To join in the blackguard throng,
    That met at Wednesbury cocking.
He borrowed a trifle of Doll,
    To back old Taverner's grey;
He laid fourpence-halfpenny to fourpence,
    He lost and went broken away.

But soon he returned to the pit,
    For he'd borrowed a trifle more money,
And ventured another large bet,
    Along with blobbermouth Coney.

When Coney demanded his money,
　　As is usual on all such occasions,
He cried, " Rot thee, if thee don't hold thy rattle,
　　I'll pay thee as Paul paid the Ephasians."

The morning's sport being over,
　　Old Spittle a dinner proclaimed,
Each man he should dine for a groat,
　　If he grumbled he ought to be maimed.
For there was plenty of beef,
　　But Spittle he swore by his troth,
That never a man should dine
　　Till he ate his noggin of broth.

The beef it was old and tough,
　　Off a bull that was baited to death,
Barney Hyde got a lump in his throat,
　　That had like to have stopped his breath,
The company all fell into confusion,
　　At seeing poor Barney Hyde choke;
So they took him into the kitchen,
　　And held him over the smoke.

They held him so close to the fire,
　　He frizzled just like a beef-steak,
They then threw him down on the floor,
　　Which had like to have broken his neck.
One gave him a kick on the stomach,
　　Another a kick on the brow,
His wife said, " Throw him into the stable,
　　And he'll be better just now."

Then they all returned to the pit,
　　And the fighting went forward again;
Six battles were fought on each side,
　　And the next was to decide the main.[1]

[1] cocking match.

For they were two famous cocks
    As ever this country bred,
Scroggins's a dark-winged black,
    And Newton's a shift-winged[1] red.

The conflict was hard on both sides,
    Till Brassy's[2] shift-winged was choked;
The colliers were tarnationly vexed,
    And the nailers were sorely provoked.
Peter Stevens he swore a great oath,
    That Scroggins had played his cock foul;
Scroggins gave him a kick on the head,
    And cried, " Fiend, fly off with thy soul."

The company then fell in discord,
    A bold, bold fight did ensue;
Bite, bludgeon and bruise was the word,
    Till the Walsall men all were subdued.
Ralph Moody bit off a man's nose,
    And wished that he could have him slain,
So they trampled both cocks to death,
    And they made a draw of the main.

The cock-pit was near to the church,
    An ornament unto the town;
On one side an old coal pit,
    The other well gorsed around.
Peter Hadley peeped through the gorse,
    In order to see the cocks fight;
Spittle jobbed out his eye with a fork,
    And said, " Rot thee, it served thee right."

[1] Probably, of two colours, light red and black, the black in broken streaks suggesting a ' shift ' or fault in a seam of coal.

[2] " Brassy " is apparently Newton's nickname, as " Spittle " is Scroggins'. That there is no explanation of this suggests that the ballad is a local one about real people.

Some people may think this strange,
  Who Wednesbury Town never knew;
But none who have ever been there,
  Will have the least doubt but it's true;
For they are so savage by nature,
  And guilty of deeds the most shocking;
Jack Baker he whacked his own father,
  And thus ended Wednesbury cocking.

# THE NIGHT BEFORE LARRY WAS STRETCHED

A Dublin street-ballad of the early nineteenth century. Two extra verses are given in Mr. Patrick Colum's *Anthology of Irish Verse*, but his version is on the whole less attractive than this, which my father, Mr. A. P. Graves, has supplied from memory. Mr. Colum notes of this ballad: " At this time there were many songs celebrating gaol life and the business of an execution. The coffin was usually sent into the condemned cell ' that the sight might suggest the immediate prospect of death and excite corresponding feelings of solemn reflection and preparation for the awful event.' The friends of the condemned man were allowed to be with him before the execution, and the coffin was generally used as a card table." The authorship of this ballad is much disputed: a scoundrelly balladist named " Harefoot Bill " is one claimant; but Francis Mahony, author of *The Bells of Shandon*, ascribes it, perhaps maliciously, to Dean Burrows.

The night before Larry was stretched,
   The boys they all paid him a visit;
A bit in their sacks[1] too they fetched,
   They sweated their duds[2] till they riz it;
For Larry was always the lad,
   When a friend was condemned to the squeezer,
But he'd fence all the togs[3] that he had
   Just to help the poor boy to a sneezer,[4]
   And moisten his gob[5] 'fore he died.

" 'Pon my conscience, dear Larry," says I,
   " I'm sorry to see you in trouble,
Your life's cheerful noggin run dry,
   And yourself going off like its bubble."

---

[1] pockets.    [2] pawned their clothes.    [3] pawn his clothes.
[4] dose of snuff.    [5] mouth and throat.

" Hould your tongue in that matter," says he;
  " For the neckcloth I don't care a button,
And by this time to-morrow you'll see
  Your Larry will be dead as mutton:
    All for what ?  'Kase his courage was good."


The boys they came crowding in fast;
  They drew their stools close round about him,
Six glims[1] round his coffin they placed;
  He couldn't be well waked[2] without 'em.
I axed, was he fit for to die,
  Without having duly repented ?
Says Larry, " That's all in my eye,
  And all by the clergy invented
    To make a fat bit for themselves."


Then the deck[3] being called for, they played,
  Till Larry found one of them cheated.
Quick! he made a hard rap at his head,
  The lad being easily heated.
" So ye chates me because I'm in grief;
  O, is that, by the Holy, the rason ?
Soon I'll give you to know, you black thief,
  That you're cracking your jokes out of sason,
    I'll scuttle your nob[4] with my fist."


Then in came the priest with his book,
  He spoke him so smooth and so civil,
Larry tipped him a Kilmainham[5] look,
  And pitched his big wig to the divil.

[1] candles.
[2] ' have a proper funeral.' This is a Lyke Wake scene very different from the Cleveland sort.
[3] pack of cards.    [4] break your head.    [5] A famous Irish gaol.

Then raising a little his head
   To get a sweet drop of the bottle,
And pitiful sighing, he said,
   " O, the hemp will be soon round my throttle,
    And choke my poor windpipe to death! "

So mournful these last words he spoke
   We all vented our tears in a shower;
For my part I thought my heart broke
   To see him cut down like a flower.
On his travels we watched him next day;
   O, the hangman, I thought I could kill him!
Not one word did our poor Larry say,
   Nor changed till he came to " King William."[1]
    Och, my dear, thin his colour turned white.

When he came to the nubbling chit,[2]
   He was tucked up so neat and so pretty;
The rumbler[3] jogged off with his feet,
   And he died with his face to the city.
He kicked, too, but that was all pride,
   For soon you might see 'twas all over;
And as soon as the noose was untied,
   Then at darky we waked him in clover,[4]
    And sent him to take a ground sweat.[5]

[1] A Dublin street.     [2] strangling cord.
[3] The cart on which he stood : when it moved away he was left hanging.
[4] i.e. at nightfall they buried him in the churchyard, where as an un-
confessed criminal he had no right to be.    [5] Blanketted him in earth.

# THE UNQUIET GRAVE

A song still sung in the West Country. It has broken away from its narrative setting, which is possibly that of *Clerk Saunders* (see *Child*), at the end of which it sometimes occurs. In other versions it is a woman who is dead, and a man who mourns her.

" Cold blows the wind on my true-love,
　　And a few small drops of rain;
I never had but one true-love,
　　And in the greenwood he lies slain.

" I'll do as much for my true-love
　　As any lover may;
I'll sit and mourn all at his grave
　　A twelvemonth and a day."

The twelvemonth and the day being gone,
　　The ghost began to greet:[1]
" Your salten tears they trickle down,
　　They wet my winding sheet."

" 'Tis I, my love, sits on your grave,
　　And will not let you sleep;
For I crave one kiss of your clay-cold lips,
　　And that is all I seek."

" O lily lily are my lips;
　　My breath comes earthy strong;
If you have one kiss of my clay-cold lips,
　　Your time will not be long.

" 'Tis down in yonder garden green,
　　Love, where we used to walk,
The finest flower that ere was seen
　　Is withered to a stalk.

[1] cry.

" The stalk is withered dry, my love,
 So will our hearts decay;
So make yourself content, my love,
 Till God calls you away."

G

# WALY, WALY

A song that has apparently broken away from the ballad of
*Jamie Douglas*. Lady Barbara Erskine, daughter of the Earl
of Mar, married James, the second Marquis of Douglas, in 1670.
There was a separation in 1681 due to a scandal of Lady Barbara's intimacy with one James Lockhart. In the ballad this
unfaithfulness is denied and the Marquis's factor, William
Lawrie, made responsible for the false charge. This song
appears first in 1727 in Ramsay's *Tea Table Miscellany*. See
*Child*.

O waly, waly,[1] up the bank!
　And waly, waly, down the brae!
And waly, waly yon burn-side,
　Where I and my love wont to gae!

I leand my back unto an aik,
　I thought it was a trusty tree;
But first it bowd, and syne it brak,
　Sae my true-love did lightly[2] me.

O waly, waly! but love be bony
　A little time, while it is new;
But when 'tis auld, it waxeth cauld,
　And fades away like morning dew.

O wherefore shoud I busk[3] my head?
　Or wherefore shoud I kame my hair?
For my true-love has me forsook,
　And says he'll never love me mair.

Now Arthur-Seat[4] shall be my bed,
　The sheets shall neer be fyl'd[5] by me;
Saint Anton's well shall be my drink,
　Since my true-love 's forsaken me.

[1] alas, alas.　　[2] treat me lightly.　　[3] dress.
[4] By Edinburgh.　　[5] soiled.

98

Martinmas wind, when wilt thou blaw,
    And shake the green leaves off the tree?
O gentle death when wilt thou come?
    For of my life I am weary.

'Tis not the frost that freezes fell,
    Nor blawing snaw's inclemency;
'Tis not sic cauld that makes me cry,
    But my love's heart grown cauld to me.

When we came in by Glasgow town,
    We were a comely sight to see:
My love was cled in the black velvét,
    And I mysell in cramasie.[1]

But had I wist, before I kissd,
    That love had been sae ill to win,
I'd lockd my heart in a case of gold,
    And pin'd it with a silver pin.

Oh, oh, if my young babe were born,
    And set upon the nurse's knee,
And I mysell were dead and gane!
    For a maid again I'll never be.

[1] crimson.

# THE HOLY LAND OF WALSINGHAME

An Elizabethan broadside. The shrine of Our Lady of
Walsingham in Norfolk was in the Middle Ages much fre-
quented by worshippers; but these pilgrimages, undertaken on
pretence of religion, were notoriously productive of love-affairs,
as Langland noted early in *Piers Plowman*. In reading this
ballad the rhythmic variations must be watched. Percy got his
version from the poet Shenstone, who had regularized the metre
throughout. The two versions may profitably be compared:
the contrast between the Elizabethan and eighteenth-century
theories of poetry will be striking.

> As ye came from the holy land
> Of Walsinghame,
> Met you not with my true love
> By the way as you came?
>
> How should I know your true love,
> That have met many a one
> As I came from the holy land,
> That have come, that have gone?
>
> She is neither white nor brown,
> But as the heavens fair;
> There is none hath her form divine
> In the earth or the air.
>
> Such a one did I meet, good sir,
> Such an angelic face,
> Who like a nymph, like a queen, did appear
> In her gait, in her grace.
>
> She hath left me here alone
> All alone, as unknown,
> Who sometime did me lead with herself,
> And me loved as her own.

What's the cause that she leaves you alone
    And a new way doth take,
That sometime did love you as her own,
    And her joy did you make?

I have loved her all my youth,
    But now am old, as you see:
Love likes not the falling fruit,
    Nor the withered tree.

Know that Love is a careless child,
    And forgets promise past:
He is blind, he is deaf when he list,
    And in faith never fast.

His desire is a dureless[1] content,
    And a trustless joy;
He is won with a world of despair,
    And is lost with a toy.

Of womenkind such indeed is the love,
    Or the word love abusèd,
Under which many childish desires
    And conceits are excusèd.

But true love is a durable fire,
    In the mind ever burning,
Never sick, never dead, never cold,
    From itself never turning.

[1] not lasting.

# LOVING MAD TOM

This ballad first appears in *Giles Earle's Song Book* in 1615, among others known to have been previously published in broadsheet form : there are many variants, from which the following version is selected. It is plainly, in the first case, written by a lettered poet, though there are verses which suggest a less cultured origin : it was certainly much sung by pretending Bedlamites in the early seventeenth century, with the second part of the second stanza as a refrain ; or with the second part of the concluding stanza. See correspondence in *London Mercury* each month from March to September, 1923.

From the hag and hungry goblin
That into rags would rend ye,
    The spirits that stand
    By the naked man
In the Book of Moons,[1] defend ye,
That of your five sound senses
You never be forsaken,
    Nor wander from
    Yourselves with Tom
Abroad to beg your bacon.

When I short have shorn my sow's face
And swigged my horny barrel,
    In an oaken inn
    I pound[2] my skin
As a suit of gilt apparel.[3]
While I sing, " Any food, any feeding,
Feeding, drink, or clothing ?
    Come, dame or maid,
    Be not afraid,
Poor Tom will injure nothing."

---

[1] An astrological treatise.      [2] possibly; impound.
[3] These five lines are either intentional gibberish or miscopied in manuscript. But the general meaning seems to be that occasionally Tom shaves his bristling chin, leaves his low drinking, and ' pounds ' or encloses himself *in* a suit of gilt apparel *at* an inn with oak panelling (not one of the poorer wattled drinking-houses).

Of thirty bare years have I
Twice twenty been enragéd,
 And of forty been
 Three times fifteen
In durance soundly cagéd,
On the lordly lofts of Bedlam,
With stubble soft and dainty,
 Brave bracelets strong ,
 Sweet whips, ding-dong,
With wholesome hunger plenty.

The Moon's my constant mistress
And the lonely owl my marrow.
 The flaming drake
 And the nightcrow make
Me music to my sorrow.
I slept not since the Conquest,
Till then I never wakéd,
 Till the roguish fay
 Of love where I lay
Me found and stript me naked.

I know more than Apollo,
For oft, when he lies sleeping,
 I see the stars
 At bloody wars
And the wounded welkin weeping,
The moon embrace her shepherd,
And the queen of love her warrior,
 While the first doth horn[1]
 The star of the morn,
And the next the heavenly farrier.[2]

---

[1] is unfaithful to.
[2] Vulcan. These references to the loves of Venus and Mars, Diana and Endymion ,are proof of this ballad's contact with classical culture.

The gipsies Snap and Pedro
Are none of Tom's comradoes;
    The punk[1] I scorn
    And the cutpurse sworn,
And the roaring-boys' bravadoes;
The meek, the white, the gentle
Me handle, touch, and spare not,
    But those that cross
    Tom Rhinoceros
Do what the panther dare not.

With an host of furious fancies,
Whereof I am commander,
    With a burning spear
    And a horse of air
To the wilderness I wander;
By a knight of ghosts and shadows
I summoned am to tourney
    Ten leagues beyond
    The wide world's end—
Methinks it is no journey.

I'll bark against the dogstar,
And crow away the morning;
    I'll chase the moon
    Till it be noon,
And I'll make her leave her horning.
But I will find bonny Maud, merry mad Maud,
I'll seek whate'er betides her,
    And I will love
    Beneath or above
That dirty earth that hides her.

[1] a wanton.

# THE CHILDREN IN THE WOOD

A Broadside Ballad of the Seventeenth Century.

### I

Now ponder well, you parents dear,
 These words which I shall write;
A doleful story you shall hear,
 In time brought forth to light.
A gentleman of good account
 In Norfolk dwelt of late,
Who did in honour far surmount
 Most men of his estate.

### II

Sore sick he was and like to die,
 No help his life could save;
His wife by him as sick did lie,
 And both possest one grave.
No love between these two was lost,[1]
 Each was to other kind;
In love they lived, in love they died,
 And left two babes behind:

### III

The one a fine and pretty boy
 Not passing three years old,
The other a girl more young than he,
 And framed in beauty's mould.
The father left his little son,
 As plainly did appear,
When he to perfect age should come,
 Three hundred pounds a year;

---

[1] This is not used in the modern satiric sense.

IV

And to his little daughter Jane
  Five hundred pounds in gold,
To be paid down on marriage-day,
  Which might not 'be controll'd.
But if the children chanced to die
  Ere they to age should come,
Their uncle should possess their wealth;
  For so the will did run.

V

" Now, brother," said the dying man,
  " Look to my children dear;
Be good unto my boy and girl,
  No friends else have they here:
To God and you I recommend
  My children dear this day;
But little while be sure we have
  Within this world to stay.

VI

" You must be father and mother both,
  And uncle, all in one;
God knows what will become of them
  When I am dead and gone."
With that bespake their mother dear:
  " O brother kind," quoth she,
" You are the man must bring our babes
  To wealth or misery!

VII

" And if you keep them carefully,
  Then God will you reward;
But if you otherwise should deal,
  God will your deeds regard."

With lips as cold as any stone,
  They kiss'd their children small:
" God bless you both, my children dear! "
  With that the tears did fall.

### VIII

These speeches then their brother spake
  To this sick couple there:
" The keeping of your little ones,
  Sweet sister, do not fear;
God never prosper me nor mine,
  Nor aught else that I have,
If I do wrong your children dear
  When you are laid in grave! "

### IX

The parents being dead and gone,
  The children home he takes,
And brings them straight unto his house,
  Where much of them he makes.
He had not kept these pretty babes
  A twelvemonth and a day,
But, for their wealth, he did devise
  To make them both away.

### X

He bargain'd with two ruffians strong,
  Which were of furious mood,
That they should take these children young,
  And slay them in a wood.
He told his wife an artful tale:
  He would the children send
To be brought up in London town
  With one that was his friend.

### XI

Away then went those pretty babes,
    Rejoicing at that tide,
Rejoicing with a merry mind
    They should on cock-horse ride.
They prate and prattle pleasantly,
    As they ride on the way,
To those that should their butchers be
    And work their lives' decay:

### XII

So that the pretty speech they had
    Made Murder's heart relent;
And they that undertook the deed
    Full sore did now repent.
Yet one of them, more hard of heart,
    Did vow to do his charge,
Because the wretch that hirèd him
    Had paid him very large.

### XIII

The other won't agree thereto,
    So here they fall to strife;
With one another they did fight
    About the children's life:
And he that was of mildest mood
    Did slay the other there,
Within an unfrequented wood—
    The babes did quake for fear!

### XIV

He took the children by the hand,
    Tears standing in their eye,
And bade them straightway follow him,
    And look they did not cry;

And two long miles he led them on,
  While they for food complain:
" Stay here," quoth he; " I'll bring you bread
  When I come back again."

### XV

These pretty babes, with hand-in-hand,
  Went wandering up and down;
But never more could see the man
  Approaching from the town.
Their pretty lips with blackberries
  Were all besmear'd and dyed;
And when they saw the darksome night,
  They sat them down and cried.

### XVI

Thus wander'd these poor innocents,
  Till death did end their grief;
In one another's arms they died,
  As wanting due relief:
No burial this pretty pair
  From any man receives,
Till Robin Redbreast piously
  Did cover them with leaves.

### XVII

And now the heavy wrath of God
  Upon their uncle fell;
Yea, fearful fiends did haunt his house,
  His conscience felt an hell:
His barns were fired, his goods consumed,
  His lands were barren made,
His cattle died within the field,
  And nothing with him stay'd.

### XVIII

And in a voyage to Portugal
Two of his sons did die;
And to conclude, himself was brought
To want and misery:
He pawn'd and mortgaged all his land
Ere seven years came about.
And now at last his wicked act
Did by this means come out.

### XIX

The fellow that did take in hand
These children for to kill,
Was for a robbery judged to die,
Such was God's blesséd will:
Who did confess the very truth,
As here hath been display'd:
The uncle having died in jail,
Where he for debt was laid.

### XX

You that executors be made,
And overseërs eke,
Of children that be fatherless,
And infants mild and meek,
Take you example by this thing,
And yield to each his right,
Lest God with suchlike misery
Your wicked minds requite.

# THE WELSH BUCCANEERS

A close and ingenious verse-rendering by Mr. A. P. Graves of a broadsheet in Welsh from the Llanddyfnan MS. (about 1652), which describes " what befel the Welsh Sea Rovers who adventured to the Indies at the behest of Elizabeth Tudor," in the year 1595. The Welsh balladist cannot escape from literary affectations even when he has a straightforward theme : nor does he tell his story quite honestly. We learn from another account of this voyage that the ten-score cannibals intent on slaughter were a few harmless islanders in bum-boats peddling fruit. There are few or no ballads extant in Welsh earlier than Tudor times ; the academic tradition hardened very early, as in ancient Ireland.

> Astray upon the Indian shore
>   It chanced that I was wandering,
> Right sadly, as the Good God knows,
>   Upon my Country pondering.
>
> When on a tree-top overhead
>   I spied through leaf and blossom
> A great fowl piercing her own breast
>   Till blood beteemed her bosom.
>
> " Good-day to thee, Dame Pelican,
>   Thou long-winged, lovely creature!
> Feeding thy brood with thine own blood,
>   So kind art thou by nature."
>
> " Good-day, likewise, to thee, my friend!
>   Whence com'st thou ?   Whither goest ?
> What dost thou here ?   For to mine eyes
>   'Tis Christianly thou showest."
>
> " A Briton and a Christian both,
>   Astray from shipmates many;
> Yet not one friend of ours, good troth!
>   Of us hath tidings any."

" Since that ye roam so far from home,
 And I am a swift sea-farer,
Unto your friends in Christendom
 I'll be your message-bearer.

" By shore and sea I'll travel free,
 The fish I catch shall feed me,
While on your errand instantly
 My waving wings shall speed me.

" But since I've ne'er in any book
 Or chart seen record written—
Must I fly forth to East or North?
 And how far off lies Britain? "

" 'Tis seventeen hundred miles away
 O'er land and sea together,
And by Platt's Rule[1] due East you'll steer,
 And prosperous be your weather!

" Then when thou comest first to land,
 To Court fly up Thames River,
And tidings true of all we do
 To our just Queen deliver.

" Unto Sir Roger Williams then,
 Mars of each battle meeting,
Beloved, incomparable Knight,
 Give our most courteous greeting.

" Say we have never seen a place,
 No island, fort, or city
Where bide the foemen of Her Grace,
 But cried to us for pity.

[1] A navigating chart.

" When first we fought on Spanish soil,
    Which our arch-foe inhabits,
We chased his ships as they had been
    But carrion crows or rabbits.

" To Porth y Saint, a puissant Isle,
    We sailed, with fire defacing
Country and town—till crack of doom
    'Tis perished past replacing.

" Beyond us from the sea outstood
    The Isles yclept the Blesséd;
The wind blew false, else were they named
    Henceforth the Isles distresséd.

" Thence far into the void we bore,
    The head-wind ne'er abating
A whole month long, till sight of land
    Relieved our anxious waiting.

" But ere we made the shore, ten score
    Of naked fiends came rowing
With painted skins and poisoned shafts
    To thwart our further going.

" Fell knaves, most rough and fierce in fight
    And Satan's spit in favour,
Their nostrils ringeｃ like rooting hogs,
    Their black jaws frothing slaver,

" Those foulest devils in God's earth—
    The Cannibals most cruel,
Brute teeth they mesh in a Christian's flesh,
    And swill his blood like gruel.

H

" Yet through that great wild host obscene,
      Intent upon our slaughter,
We brake and landed on their Isle,
      Being sore bestead for water.


" Thence in hot haste we loosed away
      And off Coetsio anchored,
Where pearls and precious stones abound,
      And that rich isle we conquered.


" To far Camenia next we steered—
      A prosperous endeavour—
Wrung ransom from the Don and took
      Three carvels on his river.


" A week thereafter, in one reach
      On lone Caractos happing,
We stormed the fort upon the beach
      And caught its keeper napping.


" Then through the country's midst we passed,
      Where foes were round us swarming,
By jungles full of trees, whose tops
      Heaven's pillar props seemed forming.


" By day and night we marched and crossed
      Great mountains—where are higher ?
Till Saint Iago's town we reached,
      The goal of our desire.


" That mighty city we besieged,
      We burned its towers to cinders;
We laid them level with the ground
      And slew their staunch defenders.

" Then we in turn were close attacked
  By hosts of stubborn Spanish;
Till desperate made from want of aid,
  At night we thence did vanish.

" Jewels and ore were here in store
  Could we have but controlled them
Yet left with thrice one hundred men,
  Too weak were we to hold them.

" For Coros next we fought a chase
  And fire thereon did scatter,
Then won its four forts sure enough
  Between the town and water.

" From out the sacking of Coros
  We shipwards bare our booty;
Though one to ten, our gallant men
  Beat back our foemen sooty;

" While some before and some behind
  And some on either flank of us
For four long hours made play—yet they
  Could never break one rank of us.

" Though in their battle rage they sped
  Amongst us poisoned arrows,
Our leaden bullets in exchange
  We launched into their marrows.

" For two long leagues we fought, fresh ground
  By force of arms still gaining,
Ere from our wounds one dart we drew
  Or thought upon their saining.

" Although our force that fought ashore
  Was but a hundred and fifty,
Thrice that tale to death we doomed,
  Not being of slaying thrifty.

" Go tell them boldly, beauteous bird,
  The Welsh are warriors splendid;
(Of Englishmen we lost a third,
  Counting both killed and wounded).

" Captain Bilins, Hector-breast,
  On land is our great guider,
In every perilous feat of arms
  He was the foremost strider.

" Captain Roberts seconds him,
  Prince Jason was no prouder;
Like great Duke Theseus with his club
  His foes he beats to powder.

" Hugh Myddleton has done his share,
  So hath each true lieutenant—
Salisbury stout and Heilin rare—
  Where'er we flew our pennant.

" Robert Bilins, Sergeant Hughes,
  Whipped the black foe like flummery!
Will Thomas, William Johnes and Hugh,
  Behold the crew of Cymry![1]

" Tell of our going to Newfoundland,
  The cruel Gulf Stream over;
'Tis thence we'll come to Christendom
  To meet fond friend and lover.

[1] Wales.

" And if too far to North we pass,
  And thereby miss our sire-land,
Then shall we sight Cape Clear aright
  And rest awhile in Ireland.

" Sure, when within your happy arms
  You nursed us, mothers loving,
I' faith how little did ye dream
  That we should thus be roving!

" Our blessings on thee, slender bird,
  If Heaven befriend thy mission,
Greet all our kin kind Wales within
  And tell them our condition."

# THE DEATH OF KING EDWARD VII

The London broadsheet in its final unhappy stage. This sort of broadsheet flourishes greatly in India to-day. When a magistrate leaves, the local pleaders and junior magistrates combine to make and print a verse-tribute, which often reads very much like this one.

The will of God we must obey.
Dreadful—our King taken away!
The greatest friend of the nation,
Mighty monarch and protection!

Heavenly Father, help in sorrow
Queen-Mother, and them to follow,
What to do without him who has gone!
Pray help! help! and do lead us on.

Greatest sorrow England ever had
When death took away our dear Dad;
A king was he from head to sole,
Loved by his people one and all.

His mighty work for the Nation,
Making peace and strengthening Union—
Always at it since on the throne:
Saved the country more than one billion.

# THE COMPLEAT HISTORY OF BOB OF LYN

A NEW BALLAD

To the tune of *Bonny Dundee*.
Proper to be sung at Elections.

This political broadsheet was published in 1916 in the
*Walpole Ballads*. The editor, Dr. Milton Percival, writes of
it : " How like you the picture of Bob of Lyn ? " inquires the
ballad. Surely the reader will like it well, however far he may
regard it from being a faithful portrait. The ballad-writer seems
to have aimed at drawing up a complete indictment, and he
certainly succeeded ; yet one or two virtues stole in unawares."
If the last stanza is a reference to the motion for Walpole's
removal, the date of the ballad cannot be earlier than the latter
part of February, 1741.
There are three other ballad biographies of Walpole : *The
Norfolk Favourite, The Statesman*, and *Appius Unmasked*.


Good People of *England !* give Ear to my Song!
It may prove of some Use, and can do you no Wrong;
Without Fear or Favour, then, here I begin;
'Tis the Birth and Adventures of *Bob of Lyn.*


*Bob of Lyn* was in Dumpling-Shire born;
Dire Omens of Halters were seen on the Morn:
Begot, as some say, by a Lawyer in Sin;
And a *promising Boy* was *Bob of Lyn.*


*Bob of Lyn* up to *Eaton* was sent;
He was apt at his Book, gave the Provost Content;
At Taw, or at Chuck, He was certain to Win;
And a *tricking young Rogue* was *Bob of Lyn.*


*Bob of Lyn* was design'd for the Gown;
But leaving the College, He came up to Town;
He took up his Lodgings in *Lincoln's-Inn* ;
And a very *great Quibler* was *Bob of Lyn.*

*Bob of Lyn* was as lusty as tall;
His Head it was large, and his Belly not small;
With huge goggle Eyes, and a soft fawning Grin:
How like you the *Picture* of *Bob of Lyn* ?


*Bob of Lyn*, tho' but small his Estate,
By his Parts, very soon, found Access to the Great:
He stood for a Borough, to the House he got in;
And thence comes the *Name* of *Bob of Lyn*.[1]


*Bob of Lyn*, Sirs, was not one of those,
Who pass all their Sessions in *Ay's* and in *No's :*
He scribbled without, and He speech'd it within;
And a bustling *M[e]mb[e]r* was *Bob of Lyn*.


*Bob of Lyn* was soon rais'd to high Post,
Of which being greedy in making the most,
He was clap'd into Durance for Brib'ry's Sin;
And a *Foraging Wight* was *Bob of Lyn*.[2]


*Bob of Lyn* now Affairs changing Face,
Triumphant once more was restor'd into Place;
But for certain sly Whispers was turn'd out again;
And a *horrid Ingrate* was *Bob of Lyn*.[3]


*Bob of Lyn*, from this faithless Event,
Became what your Courtiers do term Male-Content:
He plotted, caball'd and He thought it no Sin;
And a *furious Opposer* was *Bob of Lyn*.


[1] Walpole was member for the borough of King's Lynn.
[2] Having been found guilty of corruption with regard to two foraging contracts for Scotland, Walpole was expelled from the House and committed to the Tower (1712). This was decidedly a party proceeding, however, not merely a judicial action.
[3] Walpole followed Townshend out of office in 1717, and entered into violent opposition.

*Bob of Lyn*, by some Deaths and a Job,
Or Contract, that put near a Plumb in his Fob;
By these fortunate Hits, into Play came agen;
And rais'd to the *Helm* was *Bob of Lyn*.[1]

*Bob of Lyn*, during Twenty long Years,
Directed, perplex'd and mismanag'd Affairs:
A *Whig* out of Place, and a *Tory* when in;
And a very great *Trimmer* was *Bob of Lyn*.

*Bob of Lyn* built and purchas'd away;
And Palaces rais'd out of Houses of Clay:
He thought of nought else, when once He was in;
But hey! for the *Kindred* of *Bob of Lyn*.

*Bob of Lyn*, when the Devil did move,
Had of Concubines Store for the Banquet of Love:
Wives, Widows and Virgins, with *Peg* of the *Glyn*,
All lavishly *purchas'd* by *Bob of Lyn*.

*Bob of Lyn* so Puissant became,
He only fell short of a Monarch in Name:
He by K[ing], L[ords] and C[ommons] was held by the
    Chin;
And the *Minion of Fortune* was *Bob of Lyn*.

*Bob of Lyn* had all Law at his Will:
By magical Numbers He carry'd each Bill;
At his Nod the lawn'd Tribe[2] wou'd go thro' Thick and
    Thin;
And *Gold* was the *Wisdom* of *Bob of Lyn*.

---

[1] After the collapse of the South Sea Company (1720) Walpole was
'raised to the helm,' and put through his Bank Contract, by which he was
supposed to have pocketed 'near a plumb,' i.e. almost £100,000.
[2] The Bishops.

*Bob of Lyn* was of treating so fond,
He wou'd beg an Affront, then entreat to compound;
Still Treaties from Treaties delighted to spin;
And a very great *Blund'rer* was *Bob of Lyn.*

*Bob of Lyn* most profoundly still chose
Your Clowns and Buffoons for his sage Plenipos;[1]
For which he became of all *Europe,* the Grin;
And a very great *Bubble* was *Bob of Lyn.*

*Bob of Lyn,* tho' a Man of great Might,
Was born with a mortal Aversion to fight:
He preach'd up the sleeping in a whole Skin;
And a very *meek Christian* was *Bob of Lyn.*

*Bob of Lyn,* in the Course of his Reign,
Did Rare[e]-shew Armies and Navies maintain;
Corruption, Debts, Taxes, Excises and Gin:
These, these were the *Trophies of Bob of Lyn.*

*Bob of Lyn,* all the Wars that he made,
Were Mimickry all, and great Burthens on Trade,
He, the Honour of *England,* not valu'd a Pin;
The Merchants be *damn'd* cry'd *Bob of Lyn.*

*Bob of Lyn* was long cross'd in his Schemes,
Whose bungling Defence wasted Millions of Rheams:
He vow'd, in Revenge, He wou'd poor *England* skin;
And her *bitterest Foe* was *Bob of Lyn.*

*Bob of Lyn* now began for to fear,
In Spite of his seeming, his Reck'ning was near:
No sham Expeditions, was now all the Din;
And *loud* were the *Murmurs* 'gainst *Bob of Lyn.*

[1] "Ministers Plenipotentiary," a term invented by Walpole.

*Bob of Lyn,* 'gainst the Wishes of all,
By the Votes of the TORIES eluded his Fall:
Lend your Aid, O Electors! to drive up the Pin,
And rescue poor *Br[itai]n* from *Bob of Lyn.*

# THE PEELER AND THE GOAT

An Irish political broadsheet of penal times: printed in
Mr. Patrick Colum's *Anthology of Irish Verse.*

A Bansha Peeler wint won night
On duty and pathrollin' O,
He met a goat upon the road,
And tuck her up for strolling O.
Wud bay'net fixed he sallied forth,
An' caught her by the wizzen[1] O,
An' then he swore a mighty oath,
" I'll send you off to prison O."

"Oh, mercy, sir!" the goat replied,
" Pray let me tell my story O!
I am no Rogue, no Ribbonman,[2]
No Croppy,[3] Whig, or Tory O;
I'm guilty not of any crime
Of petty or high thraison O,
I'm sadly wanted at this time,
For this is the milkin' saison O."

" It is in vain for to complain
Or give your tongue such bridle O,
You're absent from your dwellin' place,
Disorderly and idle O.
Your hoary locks will not prevail,
Nor your sublime oration O,
You'll be thransported by Peel's Act,
Upon my information O."

[1] The weasand or windpipe.
[2] Early nineteenth-century political society, anti-Orange, mostly composed
of tenant farmers.
[3] A revolutionary society of 1798. Its members wore short hair to show
sympathy with the French Revolution.

" No penal law did I transgress
By deeds or combination O.
I have no certain place to rest,
No home or habitation O.
But Bansha is my dwelling-place,
Where I was bred and born O,
Descended from an honest race,
That's all the trade I've learned O."

" I will chastise your insolince
And violent behaviour O;
Well bound to Cashel you'll be sint,
Where you will gain no favour O.
The magistrates will all consint
To sign your condemnation O;
From there to Cork you will be sint
For speedy thransportation O."

" This parish an' this neighbourhood
Are paiceable and thranquil O;
There's no disturbance here, thank God!
An' long may it continue so.
I don't regard your oath a pin,
Or sign for my committal O,
My jury will be gintlemin
And grant me my acquittal O."

" The consequince be what it will,
A peeler's power I'll let you know,
I'll handcuff you, at all events,
And march you off to Bridewell O.
An' sure, you rogue, you can't deny
Before the judge or jury O,
Intimidation with your horns,
An' threatening me with fury O."

" I make no doubt but you are dhrunk,
Wud whiskey, rum, or brandy O,
Or you wouldn't have such gallant spunk
To be so bould or manly O.
You readily would let me pass
If I had money handy O,
To thrate you to a potheen glass——[1]
Oh! it's then I'd be the dandy O."

[1] Illegally distilled whiskey.

# BONEY

"Boney," sung by sailors as a long-drag chanty, but also popular in English country districts. John Franzwo is Jean François, the typical Frenchman.

Boney was a Warrior,
Oh, high, oh!
Boney was a Warrior,
John Franzwo!

First he beat the Prussians,
Then he beat the Russians.

Boney went to Moscow;
Moscow all a-blazing.

Boney went to Waterloo,
There he met a warrior.

He went to St. Helena,
There he was a prisoner.

Boney broke his heart and died
O, high, oh!
Boney broke his heart and died
John Franzwo.

# BLOW THE MAN DOWN

A long-drag chanty : the Black Ball Line was an English
packet fleet notorious for its brutal officers. This ballad is con-
densed from two variants in Mr. Frank Shay's *Iron Men and
Wooden Ships*.

Blow[1] the man down, bullies,[2] blow the man down
   *Way, ay—blow the man down.*
O blow the man down in Liverpool Town
   *Give me some time to blow the man down.*

'Twas on a Black Baller I first served my time
And on that Black Baller I wasted my prime.

'Tis when a Black Baller is clear of the land
Our boatswain first gives us the word of command.

" Lay aft," is the cry, " to the break of the poop
Or I'll help you along with the toe of my boot."

Then Larboard and starboard on the deck you will sprawl,
For " Kicking Jack Williams " commands that Black Ball.

'Tis when a Black Baller returns to her dock
The lassies and lads to the pierhead do flock.

Blow the man down, bullies, blow the man down.
O blow the man down in Liverpool Town.

As I was a walking down Paradise Street
A brass-bound policeman I happened to meet.

Says he, " You're a Black-baller by the cut of your hair.
I know you're a Black-baller by the clothes that you wear."

---

[1] knock.          [2] See note on *Graeme and Bewick*.

"O policeman, O policeman, you do me great wrong,
I'm a *Flying Fish* sailor just home from Hong Kong."

They gave me three months in Liverpool Town
For booting and kicking and blowing him down.

I

# JACK O' DIAMONDS

A cowboy ballad: for the music see Professor Lomax's *Cowboy Songs and other Frontier Ballads* (Fisher Unwin), a valuable collection in the introduction to which the following passage occurs: "The ranch community consisted usually of the boss, the straw-boss, the cowboys proper, the horse wrangler, and the cook—often a negro. These men lived on terms of practical equality. Except in the case of the boss, there was little difference in the amounts paid each for his services. Society, then, was here reduced to its lowest terms. The work of the men, their daily experiences, their thoughts, their interests, were all in common. Such a community had necessarily to turn to itself for entertainment. Songs sprang up naturally, some of them tender and familiar lays of childhood, others original compositions, all genuine, however crude and unpolished. Whatever the most gifted man could produce must bear the criticism of the entire camp, and agree with the ideas of a group of men. In this sense, therefore, any song that came from such a group would be the joint product of a number of them, telling perhaps the story of some stampede they had all fought to turn, some crime in which they had all shared equally, some comrade's tragic death which they had all witnessed. The song-making did not cease as the men went up the trail. Indeed, the songs were here utilized for very practical ends. Not only were sharp, rhythmic yells—sometimes beaten into verse—employed to stir up lagging cattle, but also during the long watches the night-guards, as they rode round and round the herd, improvised cattle lullabies which quieted the animals and soothed them to sleep."

O Molly, O Molly, it's for your sake alone
That I leave my old parents, my house and my home,
That I leave my old parents, you caused me to roam,—
I am a rabble soldier[1] and Dixie is my home.

Jack o' Diamonds, Jack o' Diamonds,[2] I know you of old.
You have robbed my poor pockets of silver and gold.
Whiskey, you villain, you have been my downfall,
You have kicked me and cuffed me, but I love you for all.

[1] A member of the Confederate Army.
[2] A card-game. These two lines also occur in the Negro convict ballad, *Water Boy, where are you hiding?*

My foot's in the stirrup, my bridle's in my hand.
I am going to leave sweet Molly, the fairest in the
      land.
Her parents don't like me, they say I'm too poor,
They say that I'm unworthy to enter her door.


They say I drink whiskey; my money's my own
And those that don't like me can leave me alone:
Rye whiskey, rye whiskey, rye whiskey I cry,
If I don't get rye whiskey I surely will die.


I will build me a castle on yonder mountain high
Where my true love can see me when she comes
      riding by.
Where my true love can see me and help me to
      mourn;
I am a rabble soldier and in Dixie I was born.


If the ocean were whiskey and I were a duck
I would dive to the bottom to get one sweet suck.
But the ocean's not whiskey and I'm not a duck,
So I'll play Jack o' Diamonds and drink to your good
      luck.


I have rambled and trambled this wide world around.
But it's for the rabble army, dear Molly, I'm bound.
I'll think of you, sweet Molly, you caused me to
      roam:
I am a rabble soldier and Dixie is my home.


I have rambled and gambled all my money away
And it's with the rabble army, O Molly, I must stay.
It is with the rabble army, O Molly, I must roam:
I am a rabble soldier and Dixie is my home.

Jack o' Diamonds, Jack o' Diamonds, I know you of old.
Don't rob my poor pockets of their silver and gold.
Rye whiskey, rye whiskey, rye whiskey, I cry.
If you don't give me whiskey I'll lie down and die.

# JESSE JAMES

A cowboy ballad of the 'sixties : for the music see Professor
Lomax. President Theodore Roosevelt praised *Jesse James*
highly and compared it with the Robin Hood ballads. The author,
Billy Gashade, was not, I think, proud of his authorship so much
as defiant of Robert Ford and the powers of Law and Order.

We learn from other sources that Jessie James, like the hero
of *Jack o' Diamonds,* was in the Southern Army ; when the
Civil War ended he and his brother revived it single-handed ;
or such was their excuse for their robberies and shootings. As
a patriot James had many would-be avengers ; Kelly was the
name of the successful one. Ford shot James in the back at
close range with a 42-calibre revolver while he was hanging up
a picture in his parlour at St. Louis, Missouri, where he was
living under the alias of 'Mr. Howard' (see first stanza).
Ford got 10,000 dollars reward. Kelly shot Ford while he was
charitably organizing a subscription for a sick dance-girl ; so
Ford was in turn avenged by a peace-officer.

Jesse James was a lad that killed many a man;
He robbed the Danville train.
But that dirty little coward that shot Mr. Howard
Has laid poor Jesse in his grave.

It was little Robert Ford, I wonder how he feels,
He was neither true nor brave.
For he ate of Jesse's bread and he slept in Jesse's bed,
Then laid poor Jesse in his grave.

Jesse was a man, a friend to the poor,
He would never see a man suffer pain;
And with his brother Frank he robbed the Chicago bank,
And stopped the Glendale train.

It was Jesse and Frank that robbed the Gallatin bank,
And carried the money from the town;
It was in this very place that they had a little race,
For they shot Captain Sheets to the ground.

133

They went to the crossing not very far away
And there they did the same;
With the agent on his knees, who delivered up the keys
To the outlaws, Frank and Jesse James.

It was on Wednesday night, when the moon was shining
     bright,
That they robbed the Glendale train;
The people they did say, for many miles away,
It was robbed by Frank and Jesse James.

On Saturday night, Jesse James was at home
Talking with his family brave,
Robert Ford came along like a thief in the night
And laid poor Jesse in his grave.

The people held their breath when they heard of Jesse's
     death,
And wondered how he ever came to die.
It was one of the gang called little Robert Ford,
He shot Jesse James on the sly.

Jesse went to his rest with his hand on his breast;
The devil will be upon his knee,
To welcome Jesse James to the fiery flames,
For none were as brave as he.

Jesse James had a wife, to mourn his life,
She kissed his dying face:
He was born they say in the county of Clay
And came from a solitary race.

This song was made by Billy Gashade,
As soon as the news did arrive;
He said there was no man with the law in his hand
Who could take Jesse James when alive.

# " I WANT TO GO HOME "

A ballad first noted January, 1915, in the 1st Infantry Division in France. It was current later throughout the B.E.F., but discouraged by authority. There are many more verses in the same strain. The third verse is interesting. It was composed by a junior officer in charge of machine guns and intended to raise the *morale* of the ballad: it refers to an actual German attack beaten off with loss. But as he said complainingly to me, " My men are queer: they have turned down that verse for some reason or other and refuse to sing it."

I want to go home (repeat).
The coal-box and shrapnel they whistle and roar,
I don't want to go to the trenches no more.
I want to go over the sea,
Where the Allmand can't shot[1] bombs at me.
Oh I
Don't want to die,[2]
I want to go home.

I want to go home (repeat).
I'm the bravest young man you could find in a trench.
If you don't believe me you can ask General French.
But when sausages[3] fly through the air
And there ain't no dug-out anywhere.[4]
Oh I
Don't want to die,
I want to go home.

I want to go home (repeat).
One day at Givenchy the week before last
The Allmands attacked and they nearly got past.

[1] throw (South Wales dialect).    [2] Sometimes—
                                          Oh, my!
                                          I'm too young to die!
[3] Trench-mortar shells.
[4] The Eastern war theatres added their own grievances in variants of this ballad, which was particularly popular in Palestine. One verse runs—
              " I don't like the heat, I don't like the work,
              I don't like associating with the Turk."

They pushed their way up to the Keep.
Through our Maxim-gun sights we did peep.
O My
They let out a cry!
They never got home.

# THE TOP OF THE DIXIE LID

A marching-ballad of the same date as foregoing noted in the
same battalion. The reference is to a Company Quarter-Master
Serjeant named Flavin who got decorated for bringing up rations
to the front line troops under shell-fire. The tune and words
parody a Salvation Army hymn. The Quarter-Master Serjeant
took the song in good part. For further ballads with the tunes see
Flight-Lieutenant Nettleship's *Singsongs of the War.*

Coolness under fire (repeat).
Mentioned in despatches
For pinching the Company rations,
Coolness under fire.

### Chorus.

Whiter than the whitewash on the wall (repeat).
Wash me in the water
Where you wash your dirty daughter
And I shall be whiter
Than the whitewash on the wall.

Now he's on the peg (repeat).
Mentioned in despatches
For drinking the Company rum.[1]
Now he's on the peg.

### Chorus.

Whiter than the top of the dixie-lid[2] (repeat).
Wash me in the water
Where you wash your dirty daughter
And I shall be whiter
Than the top of the dixie-lid.

---

[1] A favourite theme, e.g.—

> Do you want to find the Serjeant-Major?
> I know where he is,
> Drunk upon the dug-out floor,

and—

> If the sergeant drinks your rum, never mind.

[2] Military cooking-pan : not always particularly clean.

# TWO RED ROSES ACROSS THE MOON

A modern literary ballad by William Morris based on close
knowledge and love of the old, but altogether different in spirit.
A typical example of the part that the early ballads play in
romantic revivals.

There was a lady lived in a hall,
Large in the eyes, and slim and tall;
And ever she sung from noon to noon,
*Two red roses across the moon.*

There was a knight came riding by
In early spring, when the roads were dry;
And he heard that lady sing at the noon,
*Two red roses across the moon.*

Yet none the more he stopp'd at all,
But he rode a-gallop past the hall;
And left that lady singing at noon,
*Two red roses across the moon.*

Because, forsooth, the battle was set,
And the scarlet and blue had got to be met,
He rode on the spur till the next warm noon:—
*Two red roses across the moon.*

But the battle was scatter'd from hill to hill,
From the windmill to the watermill;
And he said to himself, as it near'd the noon,
*Two red roses across the moon.*

You scarce could see for the scarlet and blue,
A golden helm or a golden shoe;
So he cried, as the fight grew thick at the noon,
*Two red roses across the moon !*

Verily then the gold bore through
The huddled spears of the scarlet and blue;
And they cried, as they cut them down at the noon,
*Two red roses across the moon !*

I trow he stopp'd when he rode again
By the hall, though draggled sore with the rain;
And his lips were pinch'd to kiss at the noon
*Two red roses across the moon.*

Under the may she stoop'd the crown,
All was gold, there was nothing of brown;
And the horns blew up in the hall at noon,
*Two red roses across the moon.*